Uncovering the Magic of Hawaii's Isles

Ryker .F Allen

All rights reserved.

Copyright © 2024 Ryker .F Allen

Uncovering the Magic of Hawaii's Isles : Uncovering the Magic of Hawaii's Isles

Funny helpful tips:

Stay committed; dedication is key to overcoming challenges.

In the book of existence, write chapters filled with passion, purpose, and perseverance.

Life advices:

Cultivate a sense of wonder; it keeps the spirit young and vibrant.

Stay away from smoking; it has numerous detrimental effects on health.

Introduction

Welcome to this book, your ultimate resource for exploring and experiencing the wonders of this beautiful island paradise. The Big Island, also known as Hawaii Island, offers a diverse range of attractions, from stunning beaches and historic sites to breathtaking natural wonders and vibrant local culture. Whether you're seeking adventure, relaxation, or a mix of both, this guide will provide you with all the information you need to make the most of your visit.

We begin our journey in Kona, a vibrant coastal town renowned for its sunny weather, picturesque beaches, and rich history. You'll discover driving and walking tours that will take you through the charming streets of Kailua-Kona, allowing you to soak in the local culture and explore its iconic landmarks. We'll also guide you to the best beaches and parks in the Kona area, where you can unwind, swim, snorkel, or simply bask in the beauty of the surrounding landscape.

Heading south, we'll take you on a historic tour of South Kona, where you can delve into the island's rich heritage and visit significant cultural sites. If you're a coffee enthusiast, our Kona Coffee Driving Expedition will lead you through the scenic coffee farms that produce some of the world's finest beans. And don't miss out on the vibrant events and festivals happening in Kona throughout the year, where you can immerse yourself in the local traditions and celebrations.

Venturing to the Kohala region, you'll discover luxurious resorts and pristine beaches that offer a tranquil escape from the hustle and bustle of everyday life. Explore the natural beauty of the area and participate in the exciting events and festivals that showcase the unique culture and traditions of the region.

Our journey then takes us to Hilo, the capital of Hawaii Island, where you'll find a charming downtown area filled with historic buildings, local shops, and delicious eateries. Take a driving tour of Hilo to discover its hidden gems, or embark on a walking tour to immerse yourself in its vibrant atmosphere. Explore the beautiful beaches and gardens that surround Hilo, and be sure to check out the events and festivals happening in the area to experience the local culture in full swing.

No visit to the Big Island would be complete without a trip to Volcanoes National Park, where you can witness the awe-inspiring power of nature as you explore active volcanoes, lava tubes, and unique geological formations. Immerse yourself in the park's natural wonders and be captivated by the events and festivals that celebrate the island's volcanic heritage.

Venturing further, we'll guide you through the districts of Kau, Puna, and North Kohala, each offering their own unique attractions and experiences. From finding active lava flows in Puna to exploring the lush landscapes of North Kohala, you'll have the opportunity to create unforgettable memories in every corner of the island.

Driving is a popular way to explore Hawaii Island, and we provide valuable tips and estimated drive times to help you navigate the island's diverse terrain. Discover the beauty of Saddle Road and Mauna Kea, and consider exploring the nearby islands for a memorable island-hopping adventure.

Finally, we offer practical advice for planning your ideal vacation, from choosing the best time to visit to selecting the perfect accommodation and dining options. We'll also share tips for having fun and creating lasting memories during your stay on the Big Island.

Prepare yourself for an extraordinary journey as you immerse yourself in the natural wonders, rich culture, and warm hospitality of the Big Island of Hawaii. Let this guide be your companion as you explore and discover all that this enchanting island has to offer. Get ready to create unforgettable experiences and forge lasting connections with the people and the land of Hawaii Island.

Contents

CHAPTER ONE: KONA 1
    KAILUA-KONA DRIVING TOUR 3
    KAILUA-KONA VILLAGE WALKING TOUR 18
    KONA AREA BEACHES AND PARKS 36
    HISTORIC SOUTH KONA TOUR 55
    KONA COFFEE DRIVING EXPEDITION 66
    Events and Festivals in Kona 77
CHAPTER 2: KOHALA RESORTS AND BEACHES 79
    Events and Festivals near the Kohala Resorts 98
CHAPTER 3: HILO 100
    HILO DRIVING TOUR 101
    HILO DOWNTOWN WALKING TOUR 123
    HILO AREA BEACHES AND GARDENS 143
    Events and Festivals in Hilo 155
CHAPTER 4: VOLCANOES NATIONAL PARK 157
    Events and Festivals in Volcano 174
CHAPTER 5: KAU 176
CHAPTER 6: PUNA 198
    Finding Active Lava Flows 215
    Events and Festivals in Puna 217
CHAPTER 7: NORTH KOHALA 218
CHAPTER 8: WAIMEA 243
    Events and Festivals in Waimea 254
CHAPTER 9: DRIVING HAWAII ISLAND 255

Driving Tips 255
Driving Times Around the Island 257
TABLES OF ESTIMATED DRIVE TIMES 259
Saddle Road and Mauna Kea 263
Island Side Trips 266
CHAPTER 10: PLANNING YOUR IDEALVACATION 270
An Ideal Time to Visit 271
An Ideal Place to Stay 272
Where to Eat 274
Tips for Having Fun and Great Memories 274

CHAPTER ONE: KONA

Kailua-Kona from Kailua Bay

Kona has a tropical climate with dry winters and wet summers, making it a popular destination during winter months. Kona is known for its excellent snorkeling, surfing, fishing, and coffee. Fishing and ocean tour boats operate from Kona's harbor, Keauhou Bay, and Kailua Pier. The busy Kailua Bay has visiting cruise ships, the Atlantis submarine, parasailing rides, snorkel tours, and rentals for jet skis, kayaks, and paddle boards.

The Kona area is actually two districts, North Kona and South Kona. North Kona has hotels, beaches and parks from the Hualalai Resort north of Kona airport to the Sheraton Kona Resort on

Keauhou Bay. Kailua-Kona Village has the most shops, restaurants, and vibrant night life on the island. South Kona is known for its plantations, picturesque bays, and ancient Hawaiian sites.

Five maps are provided of the Kona area. Kailua-Kona is described by a driving tour with an overview of the village and a walking tour along the coast on Alii Drive. A driving tour of the coffee plantations and the historic Kealakekua and Honaunau Bays in South Kona are provided as well as descriptions of beaches and parks in North Kona.

KAILUA-KONA DRIVING TOUR

Kailua-Kona Village from Henry Street

Kailua-Kona on Kailua Bay was the home of Hawaiian Kings, the most notable King Kamehameha, who became the first ruler of all the Hawaiian Islands and established the Kingdom of Hawaii. Kamehameha was born on Hawaii Island in North Kohala and died in Kailua-Kona where the King Kamehameha Hotel is located today.

The Kailua-Kona Driving Tour is a quick overview of local beaches, businesses, and historic sites. The places can be seen from a car window, starting at the popular local beach north of Kailua Bay and ending at an area called "Hamburger Hill". More details about sites along Alii Drive between the King Kamehameha Hotel and the Royal Kona Resort are in the Kailua-Kona Village Walking Tour.

The driving tour starts at the Old Kona Airport Park. Take Kuakini Highway north until it ends. Turn left into the park and veer right to drive through a gate onto the old airport runway.

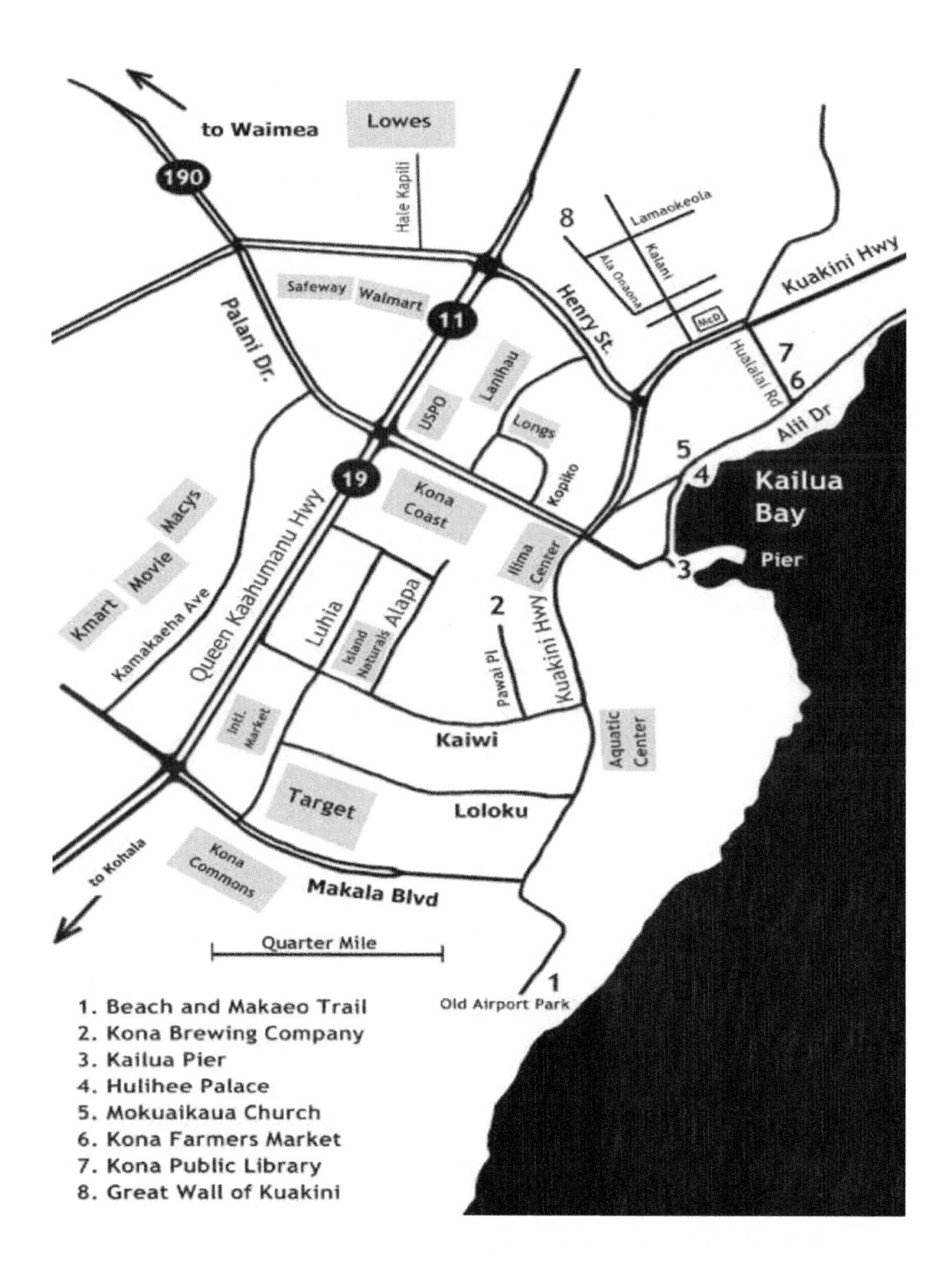

1. Beach and Makaeo Trail
2. Kona Brewing Company
3. Kailua Pier
4. Hulihee Palace
5. Mokuaikaua Church
6. Kona Farmers Market
7. Kona Public Library
8. Great Wall of Kuakini

Kailua-Kona Town Map and Driving Tour

1. Old Kona Airport Park beach and Makaeo Trail

Old Kona Airport Park Beach

The Old Kona Airport Park is a 217 acre public recreation area on Kuakini Highway. The park has a swimming pool, gymnasium, tennis courts, horseshoe pits, baseball diamonds, soccer fields, outdoor roller rink, and skateboard park. In addition to the sports facilities, the park has a mile long white sand beach along the old airport runway. At the north end of the park is a trail head into a marine life conservation area. The currents and rocky shoreline make it dangerous for swimming. The beach area has restrooms, picnic pavilions, and parking along the runway.

On the opposite side of the old runway from the beach is the community-built Makaeo walking and jogging trail. The trail loop is 0.7 miles through small, landscaped gardens planted and maintained by volunteers.

> *The Kona Airport was completed in 1949 and soon after Hawaiian Airlines started flights to Kona from Honolulu. Before the airport was built, seaplanes were used to fly passengers to Kona. The Kona Airport was used until the new airport opened in Keahole in 1970. The Queen Kaahumanu Highway (Highway 19) was built to the airport and extended to Kawaihae Bay in 1975. The runway of the old airport was used for drag racing until it was converted to a park in 1976. The old terminal building is still used as a pavilion for public events and gatherings. Radio-controlled model airplane enthusiasts use the old runway for their club meetings.* (Hawaii airport history website)

Makaeo trail is away from the noisy streets in town where it is easy to meet residents and talk story while they are tending to their gardens.

Makaeo walking and jogging trail

From the Old Kona Airport Park, take Kuakini Highway south to the Kaiwi Street intersection. Turn left on to Kaiwi and take the first right turn on to Pawai Place. The parking lot for the Kona Brewery and Pub are at the end of the street.

2. Kona Brewing Company

Kona Brewing Company (75-5629 Kuakini Hwy) was started in Kailua-Kona by Cameron Healy and his son Spoon Khalsa who introduced their beer in 1995. They have specialty beers like Longboard Island Lager and Fire Rock Pale Ale which have become popular internationally. Beer production at the Kona facility has increased every year and they now distribute it in 36 states and 10 countries. (Kona Brewing Co website)

The brewery offers tours of their operation. The Kona Pub is next to the brewery and a Growler Shack sells beer to go in half gallon glass jugs filled from the company's taps.

Kona Brewing Company, Pub, and Growler Shack

From the Kona Brewery parking lot, return to Kuakini Highway, turn left, and continue south. Turn right at Palani Road toward the ocean. After passing the King Kamehameha Hotel on the right, turn into the small turnout in front of the Kailua Pier. This area does not have parking, however the pier can be seen from the car window. To spend more time near the pier, you can park behind the hotel for a fee or use the Kailua-Kona Village Walking Tour map to find parking areas nearby.

3. Kailua Pier

Kailua Pier is the center of action in Kailua-Kona. Commercial boats for fishing, sightseeing, snorkeling, and scuba diving operate from the pier. When cruise ships arrive, local boats shuttle passengers from the ship to the pier and a US customs area is set up for thousands of visitors on international cruise ships to enter the US. The pier is also the site of canoe races, fishing tournaments where the daily catches are weighed, and Ironman triathlon competitions.

Every morning swimmers and snorkelers enter Kailua Bay at the pier to follow the Ironman route along the marked buoys in the water.

Start of Alii Drive in front of Kailua Pier turnout

The beach in front of the King Kamehameha Hotel is called Kamakahonu, which means "eye of the turtle", and is a protected cove to swim and snorkel.

Kamakahonu Beach in front of King Kamehameha Hotel

Kailua Pier was built on lava rocks in the bay in the early 1900's and upgraded in the 1950's when concrete pilings were poured. The largest rock at the base of Kailua Pier is called "Plymouth Rock" because the first Christian missionaries to Hawaii landed at that spot.

The first company of New England missionaries arrived at "Plymouth Rock" in March 1820, less than a year after the death of King Kamehameha and just a few months after a major battle, the Battle of Kuamoo, which put an end to the Hawaiian Kapu religion. The missionaries from Massachusetts were given permission to stay in Hawaii by Liholiho, King Kamehameha II, who lived in Kailua-Kona. Asa and Lucy Thurston remained to minister to the royal family while the rest of the missionaries continued on to Honolulu. (Thurston, 1882)

From the Kailua Pier turnout, on the corner of Palani Road and Alii Drive, continue the tour on Alii Drive along the sea wall. At the end of the seawall, the Hulihee Palace is on the right side.

4. Hulihee Royal Palace

Hulihee Palace from Alii Drive

Hulihee Palace (75-5718 Alii Drive) is a two story New England style residence built in 1838 by Kuakini, the second Governor of the Island of Hawaii. Kuakini was responsible for many major construction projects in the Kona area including the Mokuaikaua Church across the street from his residence and the Great Wall of Kuakini.

After Kuakini died, his estate changed ownership many times. It became a palace when King David Kalakaua and his wife became the owners and made major upgrades to the estate. The Palace is now a museum run by the Daughters of Hawaii with ancient Hawaiian artifacts, original furniture, and personal items owned by the royal family. (Hulihee Palace website)

Kuakini was the son of High Chief Keeaumoku who was King Kamehameha's most trusted chief and responsible for his first victory at the Battle of Mokuohai in 1782. Three of Kuakini's sisters were married to King Kamehameha, who had many wives. Kuakini gained power when his sister Queen Kaahumanu became the regent of the Kingdom after King Kamehameha's death.

Kuakini changed his name to John Adams and adopted American clothing and customs. He was described as being 6 feet 3 inches tall, weighed over 400 pounds, and had a powerful presence. He served as the second Governor of Hawaii Island until his death in 1844. (Ellis, 1827)

The Mokuaikaua Church can be seen across Alii Drive from Hulihee Palace.

5. Mokuaikaua Church

Mokuaikaua Church (75-5713 Alii Drive) was the first stone church in Hawaii. It was built by Governor Kuakini for Asa Thurston's congregation in 1837. The stones for the church were collected from a destroyed temple near the pier. The church's crushed coral and lava walls and its steeple, which has become a symbol of Kailua-Kona, can be seen from Alii Drive. (Mokuaikaua Church website)

On October 23, 1819, Asa and Lucy Thurston, six other missionary couples, 5 children, and 4 Hawaiian youths boarded the ship Thaddeus in Boston for a 6 month voyage to Kailua-Kona. Their trip was inspired by Henry Opukahaia, a young Hawaiian who had fled the wars on Hawaii Island in 1808 by signing up as a cabin boy on an American ship in Kealakekua Bay. Henry joined the Foreign Missions School in Connecticut, became the first Hawaiian Christian, and wrote a book about the violence and Kapu religion in Hawaii. Opukahaia's death in 1818 and the publication of his book motivated the missionaries to come to Hawaii. The first company of New England missionaries expected to be rejected or even killed by the powerful priests of the Hawaiian Kapu religion.

Mokuaikaua Church from Alii Drive

    The Thaddeus arrived in Kawaihae on Hawaii Island on March 30, 1820. A ship's officer and two Hawaiian missionaries went ashore to meet with John Young, an advisor to King Kamehameha. The missionaries waited in suspense on the ship. Lucy Thurston described the amazing news brought by the ship officer: "Kamehameha is dead; - his son Liholiho is King; - the Kapus are abolished; - the images are burned; - the temples are destroyed. There has been war. Now there is peace."

    Chief Kalanimoku, the head of the royal army, had been victorious at the Battle of Kuamoo three months earlier where an army supporting the Kapu religion had been defeated. Kalanimoku was at Kawaihae and requested passage on the Thaddeus to Kailua-Kona. Kalanimoku later became the Prime Minister of Hawaii Kingdom and took the name William Pitt. He boarded the ship with two widow Queens of King Kamehameha and the missionaries joyfully continued their voyage. Lucy Thurston described the widow Queens as being at least 300 pounds and *wearing only a cloth made of kapa bark wrapped around their hips. The two widow Queens requested dresses made of cloth like the missionary women wore. The missionary wives sewed them dresses with cloth they had brought on the journey. The Thaddeus landed at Kailua-Kona on April 4, 1820. (Thurston, 1882)*

Continue on Alii Drive past the Kona Inn Shopping Village on the right side. Turn left, after Uncle Billy's Kona Bay Hotel on the left, on to Hualalai Road. Farmer's Market is on the right.

6. Kona Farmer's Market

Kona Farmers Market on Alii Drive and Hualalai Road

Kona Farmer's Market is in a parking lot at the intersection of Alii Drive and Hualalai Road. The outdoor market has over forty vendors selling island produce, food, flowers, and crafts. The market is open every week from Wednesday to Sunday. The entrance to the parking lot is on Hualalai Road. (Kona Farmer's market website)

Above the Farmer's Market, on Hualalai Road, is Kona's library.

7. **Kona Public Library**

Kona Public Library

The Kailua-Kona Public Library (75-138 Hualalai Road) opened in February 1992 and is the second largest on Hawaii Island. The library is a popular place for residents to read and relax. Book club meetings and events are open to visitors and held on the lanai that overlooks the Farmer's Market and Kailua Bay. The library is closed Sundays and Mondays. A monthly book sale is run by the Friends of the Library. (Kona Library friends website)

A section of Kuakini's Wall is the last place on the tour. It is on "Hamburger Hill", the local name of the area above the McDonalds restaurant on Kuakini Highway. From the library, on Hualalai Street, drive to the intersection at Kuakini Highway and turn left. Then turn right on to Kalani Street just past McDonalds. Drive up the hill on Kalani Street to the third street from Kuakini Highway and turn left on to Lamaokeola Street. At the end of the road turn right on to Ala Onaona Street. A plaque is located where the street ends.

8. Great Wall of Kuakini

The Great Wall of Kuakini (Ka Pa Nui o Kuakini) was built in the 1830's and extended from Kailua to Keauhou. The wall took 10 years to build with lava rocks up to 6 feet tall and 4 feet wide. Its purpose was to separate the inland pastures from the coast to keep cattle and wild animals from wandering into the villages.

Cattle were originally brought to Hawaii Island in 1793 by Captain Vancouver. They quickly multiplied because hunting them was not allowed and punishable by death. Within 30 years, thousands of wild cattle roamed the island, trampled the crops, and terrorized the people.

A plaque and section of Kuakini's Wall

Kuakini's Wall was built using dry-stack stone masonry or "Uhau humu pohaku" which is a method of stacking and locking stones together to form structures without cement or cutting. Walls and structures constructed with this method can be seen at many historic sites around the island.

KAILUA-KONA VILLAGE WALKING TOUR

The distance along Alii Drive from the King Kamehameha Hotel (Courtyard by Marriott) to the Royal Kona Resort is about one mile. The walk has fantastic ocean views with shops, restaurants, churches, and museums along the route. The sidewalk is flat with many places under shade trees to rest and enjoy the view.

The Kailua-Kona Village Map shows parking areas near Alii Drive. The parking lot behind the King Kamehameha Hotel is the closest to the pier, however there is a fee to park there. During holidays and festivals, parades use the Alii Drive route and once a month a portion of Alii Drive is closed to vehicles for a village stroll. This walking tour starts on the beach in front of the King Kamehameha Hotel in an area called Kamakahonu.

Sidewalk along the seawall in Kailua-Kona

The Honu Trolley is another way to get around Kona. There is a fee to ride the trolley between its stops in Kona and Keauhou. Its route is from the Sheraton Kona Resort in Keauhou to Kailua Pier and up to Kona's shopping areas near Highway 19. The lime green trolley can often be seen parked under the huge Banyan tree in the turnout in front of Kailua Pier.

Honu Bus by Kailua Pier

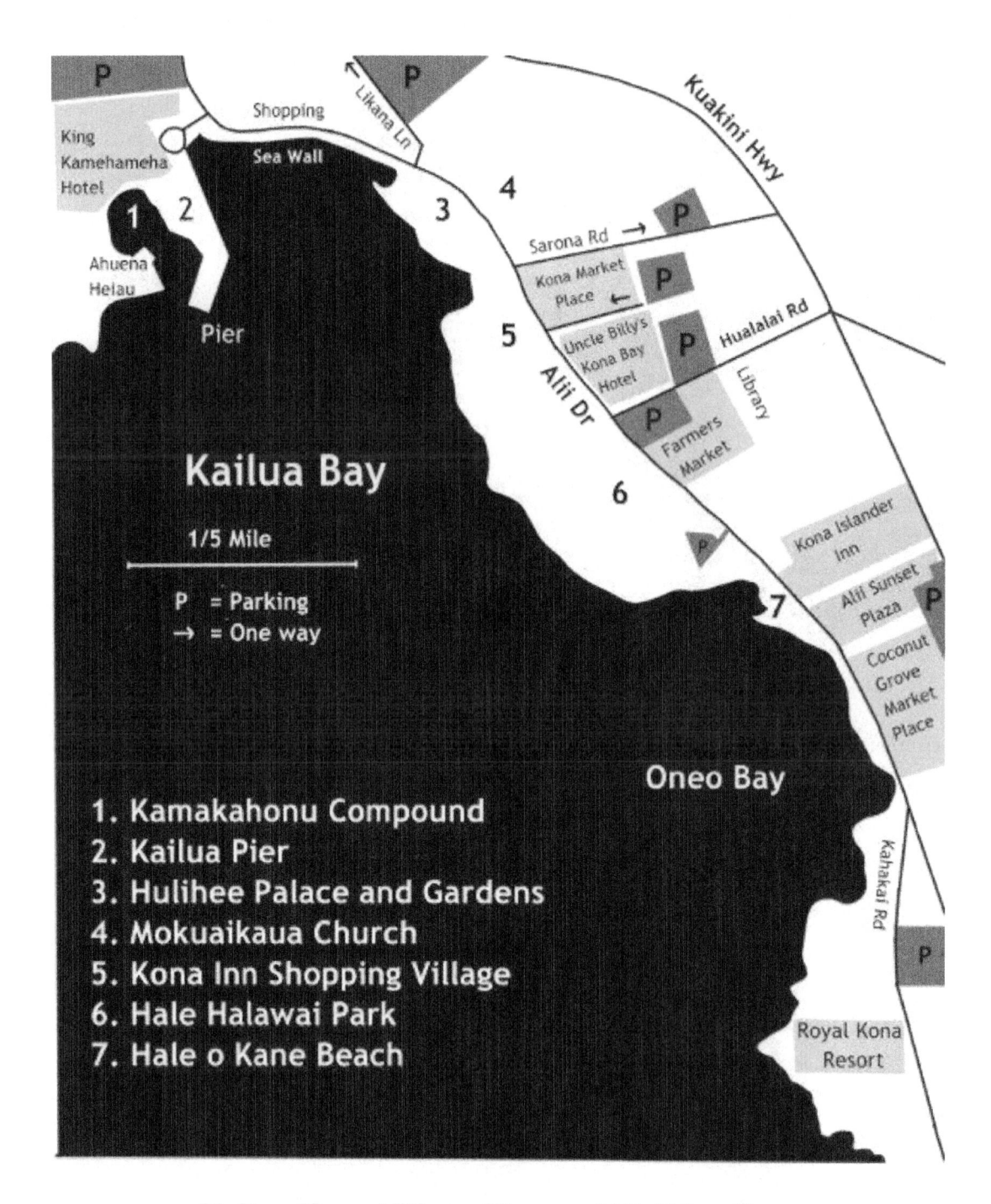

Kailua-Kona Village Map and Walking Tour

1. Kamakahonu Compound
2. Kailua Pier
3. Hulihee Palace and Gardens
4. Mokuaikaua Church
5. Kona Inn Shopping Village
6. Hale Halawai Park
7. Hale o Kane Beach

1. Kamakahonu Compound

Kamakahonu, meaning the "eye of the turtle", is the name of the area around the King Kamehameha Hotel and Kailua Pier. It was the first capital of the Kingdom of Hawaii where King Kamehameha resided in his last years and his son, Liholiho, King Kamehameha II, began his reign. Kamehameha also lived near Kamakahonu as a chief and warrior when his uncle, King Kalaniopuu ruled the island.

Kamakahonu Cove and Ahuena Heiau

The Ahuena Heiau (heiau means temple in Hawaiian) was a complex located in front of the King Kamehameha Hotel. The original temple extended into the bay beyond where Kailua Pier is today with massive lava rock walls surrounded by carved statues.

(James, 1995) A replica of the Ahuena Heiau was completed in 1977 from sketches by Louis Choris who visited Kailua-Kona in 1816 on the Russian ship Ruric. The replica, located on the north end of the cove, is smaller than the original size with a wicker alter, tower and carved figures. (Ahuena Heiau website) The grassy area in front of the temple is used for luaus. Hawaiian art exhibits and other historic items are displayed in the lobby of the King Kamehameha Hotel. (King Kamehameha Hotel website)

King Kamehameha returned to Kailua-Kona in 1812 after conquering Oahu. He restored and rededicated the Ahuena Heiau to Lono, the god of peace, agriculture, and prosperity. (James, 1995) In his last years he instructed his teenage son Liholiho (King Kamehameha II) and had another son Kauikeaouli (Kamehameha III) who was born in nearby Keauhou in 1813. Maps by Henry Kekahuna show Kamakahonu cove lined with eighteen 32-pound cannons to protect the area. King Kamehameha died at his home in Kamakahonu in May 1819. The Hawaiian temples, like Ahuena, were ordered destroyed after Kamehameha's death when the Hawaiian Kapu religion was abolished by Liholiho and the regent Queen Kaahumanu.

From the King Kamehameha Hotel beach, walk over to the pier.

2. Kailua Pier and Seawall

Kailua Pier entrance

At the front the Kailua Pier are restrooms and showers on the right. Bike racks and shelves, next to the small beach entrance, are on the left where swimmers and snorkelers leave their belongings while swimming along the Ironman route marked with buoys. Walking on the pier, a US Customs area is set up on the left side when cruise ships are docked in the bay. Tour operators for Atlantis submarine, UFO parasailing, Body Glove and other tours are located along both sides of the pier. At the end of the pier, the front of the Ahuena temple can be seen. The property next to the temple, on the other side of a stone wall, has a fishpond, garden, and a large estate. This was once the estate of Lorrin P. Thurston, the great grandson of the first missionaries to Kailua-Kona, Asa and Lucy Thurston. The property is now owned by Paul Allen, co-founder of Microsoft, whose mega-yacht can be seen near the pier when he visits.

From Kailua Pier follow the wide sidewalk next to the rock seawall. Restaurants and stores are on the other side of Alii Drive. Sometimes waves splash over the seawall, drenching unsuspecting people on the sidewalk.

Umi Rock under Sea Wall in Kailua-Kona Village

Halfway between the pier and the end of the seawall on Alii Drive is a prominent point of lava rock called Pao Umi Rock. This is the spot where King Umi (Umi-a-Liloa) is said to have landed in the 1500's when he first came to Kailua-Kona by canoe from his royal court in Waipio. King Umi moved the royal court to Kailua-Kona near this landing point. The rock is barely visible under the seawall, but can be seen from Hulihee Palace grounds.

King Umi's life and exploits have been kept alive in Hawaiian chants and oral history. Umi was raised in Hamakua, north of Hilo, by his mother and her husband not knowing that he was the son of King Liloa from a chance encounter his mother had with the King. When Umi was a young man, his mother gave him the keepsakes that Liloa had given her to make the child known to him and told him how to get to the royal court in Waipio Valley. Umi snuck into the royal compound and sat in the King's lap. After recovering from the shock, the King recognized the items Umi brought and acknowledged him as his son. When King Liloa died, Umi's older brother Hakau became King and was hated for his cruel treatment of the people. Umi overthrew him and became a popular ruler of Hawaii Island. He moved the royal court to Kona and is credited with a new form of farming called the Kona Field System which increased the production of food on the dry, west side of the island. (Fornander, 1916)

Umi ruled hundreds of years before contact with Europeans was recorded. However, there are signs of Western influences during Umi's time. There are mysterious crosses made with mosaic pavements in temples built by Umi. The symbol of a cross has not been found in any structures or temples before or after Umi's time. There is also evidence that Spanish ships discovered the Hawaiian Islands long before Captain Cook. Spanish archives have charts from the 1500's that show islands in the area of Hawaii. Hawaii Island is named "La Mesa" (the table), and Maui, "La Desgraciada", (the unhappy), and islands resembling Lanai, Molokai and Kahoolawe are named "Los Monjes" (the monks). (Taylor, 1922)

At the end of the sidewalk along the seawall there is a small white sand beach where the seawall curves away from Alii Drive. This beach borders the grounds of Hulihee Palace. Follow the seawall onto the Hulihee Palace grounds where the seawall continues along the coast behind the Palace.

3. Hulihee Palace Museum and Grounds

Seawall behind Hulihee Palace grounds

The Hulihee Palace grounds have interesting artifacts in the garden. A concrete slab marks the location where a British group set up an auxiliary station to observe the 1874 transit of Venus. A Konane board (Hawaiian checkers game) and Petroglyph stone are also on the grounds.

Hulihee Palace grounds

Governor Kuakini built Hulihee Palace in 1838 to use as his residence after he completed the Mokuaikaua Church across the street. The estate became a retreat for the royal family and eventually a secondary palace when it was purchased by King David Kalakaua and his wife Queen Kapiolani.

The house is now a museum with original furnishings including King Kalakaua's dining table and writing desk and Queen Kapiolani's sandalwood wardrobe. There are portraits, royal memorabilia, and special items such as King Kamehameha's 22-foot spear inlaid with ivory on display. The museum and gift store are open Tuesday through Saturday and closed on major holidays. The museum charges a fee. (Hulihee Palace website)

Princess Ruth Keelikolani inherited the Hulihee estate after her husband, the adopted son of Kuakini, died at 22 years of age. Though her bedroom has many of her personal items, she slept in a grass house on the grounds rather than in Hulihee. She used the house for entertaining royal visitors for 40 years. (huliheepalace.net)

Princess Ruth was said to have had a powerful presence and massive size. One of her famous acts was saving Hilo in 1881 from a Mauna Loa lava flow. She started up the hill from Hilo Bay in her carriage. The horse could not pull her weight so prisoners from Hilo jail were used to push her carriage up to the edge of the lava flow. She threw 30 red silk handkerchiefs and a bottle of brandy into the lava and prayed to Pele, the volcano goddess, for Hilo's safety. The lava came to a halt a few days later within a mile and a half of Hilo Bay. (Oaks, 2003)

From Hulihee Palace walk across Alii Drive to the Mokuaikaua Church entrance.

4. Mokuaikaua Church

Mokuaikaua Church Entrance

    The cornerstones of Mokuaikaua Church were laid in January 1836 and the building was completed a year later. Lava rocks were cemented with white coral mortar and the posts and beams are made of ohia wood. The 112 foot steeple was the highest structure in Kona for many years and used as a landmark by ships. The stone arch in front was built in 1910 to commemorate the 90th anniversary of the missionaries arrival to Hawaii.

    Inside the church, the pews, pulpit, railings, and panels are made of koa wood using wooden notches and pegs. At the back of the church is a small museum with a model of the ship Thaddeus and pages from Lucy Thurston's diary. (Mokuaikaua Church website)

Brig Thaddeus inside Mokuaikaua Church

After arriving in Kailua-Kona in 1820, the Thurstons lived and taught in a thatched house provided by the King. A larger church was constructed in 1825 that burned down in 1835, where Mokuaikaua Church stands today. (Thurston, 1882)

Kamehameha's most powerful wife, Queen Kaahumanu had a house next to the Mokuaikaua Church. She was born on Maui; her mother was related to the Kings of Maui. She moved to Hawaii Island as a baby where her father became a powerful chief and she was wed to Kamehameha as a teenager. Although she had no children, she was the King's favorite wife and became Regent of the Kingdom, "Kuhina Nui", after King Kamehameha's death. As Regent, she engineered the overthrow of the Kapu religion and later became a Christian. (Desha, 2000)

From the church, walk across the street to the ocean side of Alii Drive. The Kona Inn Shopping Village is on the right, just beyond

Hulihee Palace grounds.

5. Kona Inn Shopping Village

Kona Inn Shopping Village and boardwalk

The Kona Inn Shopping Village (75-5744 Alii Drive) has specialty shops and ocean front restaurants with an interior boardwalk. There is a large grassy area in front of the seawall next to the Kona Inn restaurant accessible from the boardwalk.

The old Kona Inn was Kona's first hotel built in 1928 by the Inter-island Steam Navigation Company. According to maps by Henry E. P. Kekahuna, before the hotel was built, the property had four houses owned by the King, a temple, and a spring. The Kona Inn had 20 rooms, a restaurant, and large lanai overlooking the bay that attracted fishermen and tourists. The inn was closed in the 1970's but the restaurant is still open. Old photographs of Kona and other memorabilia are located in the Kona Inn restaurant lobby. (Kona Inn restaurant website)

Sea wall and grounds behind Kona Inn Shopping Village

6. Hale Halawai Park

Hale Halawai park and pavillion

Hale Halawai is an oceanfront park on Alii Drive next to the Kona Inn Shopping Village. In the center of the park is the Hale Halawai pavilion which is used for community events and classes. A police substation is also located in the building.

Across the street from the Hale Halawai park is the Kona Farmer's Market. Next to the Farmer's Market is the property of St Michael the Archangel Catholic Church founded in 1840 and dedicated in 1850. The church was badly damaged during the 2006 earthquake and had to be demolished. A new church is currently under construction.

Walking south, past the Hale Halawai parking lot, is a building with a blue roof called Waterfront Row. There is a parking garage under the building. The Bubba Gump restaurant is located next to

Waterfront Row. A small beach on Alii Drive is further south on the walk, across from the Kona Islander Inn.

7. Hale o Kane Beach

Hale o Kane grounds of Kealaokamalamalama Church

Hale o Kane is a fenced grass area that was part of the Kealaokamalamala Church. The church was founded in 1934 by Reverend Francis K. Akana and later demolished. Services are held on this grassy area in front of the ocean.

Beyond Hale o Kane beach is Oneo Bay. The Alii Sunset Plaza and Coconut Grove Marketplace are across Alii Drive from Oneo Bay with shops, restaurants, and bars. A large parking lot is located behind the retail area off Kuakini Drive. The Outback Steak House, Lava Java, Humpy's, Subway, Lulu's, and other restaurants attract crowds from early morning for coffee until late at night when the bars close. At the end of Oneo Bay is the Royal Kona Resort just a short walk from Alii Drive past Huggo's ocean front restaurants.

Oneo Bay and the Royal Kona Resort

The Royal Kona Resort was built in 1968 as a Hilton. It is known for its ocean front dining and Don the Beachcomber Mai Tai festival in August. The hotel is a popular place to watch canoe races and fishing competitions in Kailua Bay. (Royal Kona Resort website)

KONA AREA BEACHES AND PARKS

This section has a map and directions to great beaches, gardens, parks, and historical sites that are near Kailua-Kona Village in the district of North Kona. It covers the area from Hualalai Resort, north of Kona's Keahole Airport, to Keauhou Bay, south of Kailua-Kona Village.

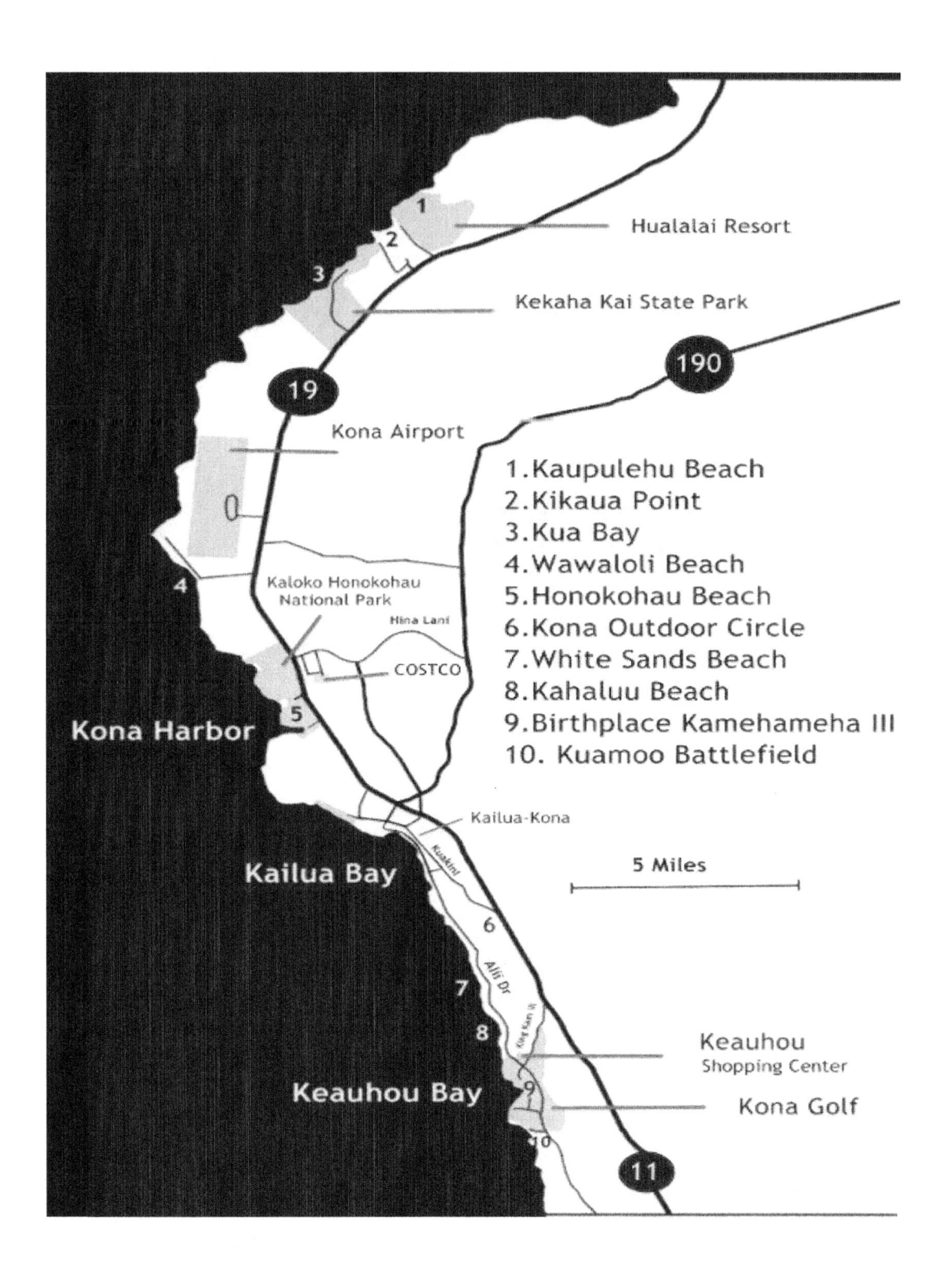

1. Kaupulehu Beach
2. Kikaua Point
3. Kua Bay
4. Wawaloli Beach
5. Honokohau Beach
6. Kona Outdoor Circle
7. White Sands Beach
8. Kahaluu Beach
9. Birthplace Kamehameha III
10. Kuamoo Battlefield

North Kona Beaches, Gardens, and Parks

1. Kaupulehu Beach

Kaupulehu Beach in front of Four Seasons Hotel

Kaupulehu Beach is a white sand beach in the Hualalai Resort. A paved path along the beach, in front of the Four Seasons Hotel, is great for walking. The beach is not a safe for swimming. The Four Seasons Hotel is 6.3 miles north of Kona's Keahole airport on Highway 19. Turn toward the coast on Kaupulehu Drive. The north lot of the hotel has a few public parking spots within walking distance of the beach. (Four Seasons Hualalai website)

The Kaupulehu area around the Four Seasons was once the site of a large fishing village called Manuahi. In 1790 an American ship, the Eleanora, moored in the bay and met with a Kona chief named Kameeiamoku. Captain Simon Metcalfe was in Hawaii for the winter during a fur trading voyage to China. The meeting with the chief went badly and for some unknown reason Metcalfe had him whipped and then sailed for Maui where he became infamous for the massacre of a village with his cannon. About a month later, Metcalf's son Thomas, captain of the schooner Fair American that accompanied the Eleanora, arrived at

Manuahi on his way to Kealakekua Bay where he planned to meet the Eleanora. The Kona chief was still furious over his treatment and attacked the Fair American. Four of the five crew were killed, including Metcalfe's 19 year old son. Isaac Davis survived but he was seriously injured. When Metcalfe's son did not show up in Kealakekua Bay, John Young was sent ashore to ask the whereabouts of the Fair American. Kamehameha had heard of the schooner's demise and held John Young captive. Metcalf eventually continued on to China without knowing what happened to his son. Kamehameha spared the lives of Davis and Young and they became his advisors and helped him win battles with the cannon from the Fair American using western battle tactics. During Kamehameha's reign, Davis and Young became high chiefs, diplomats, and island governors. (Desha, 2000)

The fishing village was destroyed in 1800 by an eruption of Hualalai Volcano. The lava flow covered the large bay and fishponds and the deserted area was renamed to Kaupulehu. John Young witnessed the destruction and told a visiting missionary that numerous offerings were made to appease the gods and stop the devastating flow. Nothing worked until Kamehameha cut off a piece of his hair and threw it in the lava. A day or two later the lava flow stopped. (Ellis, 1827)

2. Kikaua Point

Kikaua Point Beach at Kukio

Kikaua Point is in front of the Kukio residential community south of the Four Seasons. The man-made beach has white sand and shaded, grassy areas. A small cove surrounded by lava rock provides a protected swimming area. There are no lifeguards and currents are dangerous beyond the cove. A paved path leads from the parking lot to the beach where restrooms and showers are located.

Parking for Kikaua Point is limited to 20 cars. Parking passes are given by guards at a gate on Kukio Nui Drive. Kukio Nui Drive is located off Highway 19, just south of Kaupulehu Drive, 6 miles from Keahole Airport Road.

3. Kua Bay in Kekaha Kai State Park

Entrance to Kekaha Kai State Park to Kua Bay

Kua Bay, called Maniniowali Beach, is located in Kekaha Kai State Park. The bay is known for its turquoise color and gorgeous white sand beach. The beach also has a great view of the open ocean where whales can be seen in season.

A paved entrance to the parking lot, directly across from the West Hawaii Veterans Cemetery, is located on Highway 19 between the 88 and 89 mile markers and 4.6 miles north of Keahole Airport Road. The park has picnic tables, restrooms, and showers. There are no life guards.

Turquoise colored water of Kua Bay

The path to the beach from the parking lot is rough with sharp lava. Kua Bay is best early in the day when it is less crowded and the surf is calmer. Surf conditions can make swimming hazardous during storms and winter swells.

4. Wawaloli Beach Park

Wawaloli Beach at the Natural Energy Lab

Wawaloli Beach is located in the Natural Energy Laboratory of Hawaii just south of the airport. The rocky shoreline has tidal pools and some areas of white sand. Although it is not a good area for swimming, the shallow, protected tidal ponds are popular with families.

The beach is accessible on Makako Bay Drive, the entrance road to the Natural Energy Laboratory of Hawaii (NELHA) on Highway 19, just south of Keahole Airport Road. The beach starts where Makako Bay Drive curves north at the shore. The beach facilities include restrooms and showers.

The Natural Energy Laboratory was funded by the State Legislature to study alternative forms of energy and ocean thermal energy conversion. A polyethylene pipe that extends 2000 feet down into the ocean collects cold, pure water that is used by companies within the NELHA facility for bottled drinking water and aquaculture. Companies raising Abalone, Seahorses, and Lobsters are located on Makako Bay Drive and offer tours of their operations for a fee. (Kona Energy Lab website)

---

5. Honokohau Beach and National Park

Honokohau Beach in Kaloko-Honokohau National Park

Honokohau Beach is in Kaloko-Honokohau National Historical Park. The beach has a restored canoe house and an ancient stone fish trap. The Aiopio fish trap allows fish to swim in at high tide and traps them in the stone enclosure at low tide. Snorkeling and sun bathing are popular at this beach.

The entrance gate to Honokohau Beach is within Kona Honokohau Boat Harbor on Kealakehe Parkway. Kealakehe Parkway is 4.6 miles south of Keahole Airport Road on Highway 19. Turn into the harbor at Kealakehe Parkway and turn right at the first intersection. Drive to the end of the road where a gate to the national park is on the right and a large parking lot on the left. A rocky trail leads from the park gate to the beach.

Aiopio Fish trap

An alternate walk back to the parking lot is from the south end of Honokohau Beach near Mailu Point where a gate leads to the harbor channel.

Kona Honokohau Small Boat Harbor

Kona Honokohau Boat Harbor serves tour operators, fishing boats, and private yachts. You can watch the fishermen weigh their catch and also purchase fish at the market. The harbor basin and channels were completed in 1970 by the Army Corp of Engineers. Restrooms, shops, and restaurants, are located at the harbor. (Honokohau Harbor website)

Kaloko Honokohau National Park Visitors Center

The Visitor's Center for the 1160 acre Kaloko-Honokohau National Historical Park is located a half mile north of the harbor entrance at Kealakehe Parkway. It has a large parking area, restrooms, and a small store. There is a park ranger at the Visitors Center and maps are available. (Kaloko-Honokohau National Historical Park website)

6. Kona Outdoor Circle and Botanical Garden

Sadie Seymore Botanical Garden

Kona Outdoor Circle (76-6280 Kuakini Hwy) was organized to preserve and beautify Kona. The Sadie Seymour Botanical Garden is located on the property as well as a Hawaiian temple built by King Umi used to bless canoes. The botanical garden was designed by Scott Seymour and named in honor of his mother, the founder of Kona Outdoor Circle. The center has gardening classes and a thrift shop located in the basement. (Kona Outdoor Circle website)

    The Kona Outdoor Circle Educational Center and garden are located at the intersection of Highway 11 and Kuakini Highway, south of Kailua-Kona.

7. White Sands Beach

    White Sands Beach has many names. It is called Laaloa Beach Park as well as Disappearing Sands Beach and Magic Sands Beach. It is the closest surfing and boogie boarding beach to Kailua-Kona and has the most white sand along the coast between Kailua-Kona and Keauhou. During heavy storms the white sand "magically" disappears and exposes the rocky shore.

White Sands Beach Park

    The beach's parking lot is 4 miles south of the King Kamehameha Hotel on Alii Drive. There are restrooms, showers, and lifeguards. The site of a Hawaiian temple called Leleiwi (bone altar) is next to the beach.

8. Kahaluu Beach Park

Kahaluu Beach Park

Kahaluu Beach is a popular place for snorkeling in Kona. The protected bay has a reef where turtles and colorful fish live within a stone breakwater wall. Volunteers are often at the beach to answer questions about the fish and turtles. The northern edge of the bay, outside the breakwater, is popular with surfers. There are powerful currents outside the breakwater.

Kahaluu's parking lot is 5 miles south of the King Kamehameha Hotel on Alii Drive. The park has restrooms, showers, a covered picnic area, and lifeguards.

The wall enclosing Kahaluu Bay is called Paokamenehune which means "Menehune breakwater". The Menehune are a legendary race of small people in Hawaii who are credited for the construction of walls and structures in a single night. It is said that if the Menehune are interrupted or cannot complete a project in one night, then it is never finished. The wall was originally a semicircle 3900 feet long. (James, 1995)

Kuemanu Temple near Kahaluu Bay

The stone platform of a surfing temple, Kuemanu Heiau, where chiefs prayed for good surfing conditions, is located on the north side of Kahaluu Bay on Alii Drive. The tiny St. Peter's by the Sea Catholic Church is next to it. The little blue church was originally built in 1880 across from White Sands Beach and moved in 1912 to its current location.

The missionary William Ellis published an account of his tour of Hawaii Island in 1823. He counted 19 temples on his 8 mile walk from Kailua-Kona village to Keauhou Bay. The stretch of Kona coastline from Kailua Pier to the Puuhonua o Honaunau National Historical Park was once considered the most sacred area of the island. (Ellis, 1827)

Two temples, Keeku and Hapaialii Heiaus, are located south of Kahaluu Bay next to the shuttered Keauhou Outrigger Hotel. The Hapaialii Heiau has been carbon-dated to the early 1400's. At very low tide, petroglyphs carved into the pahoehoe lava are visible and one of them is said to be a likeness of Maui Chief Kamalalawalu who attacked Kona and was sacrificed at the Keeku Heiau after being defeated.

(James, 1995) You can visit the temples, which are on Kamehameha Schools land, by asking permission at the gate just past the Keauhou sign on Alii Drive.

Keauhou Bay means "the new era" and is 1.5 miles south of Kahaluu Bay on Alii Drive. The bay is used for snorkel tours, dive boats, kayak rentals, and home to the Keauhou Canoe Club. There is limited parking available at the end of the King Kamehameha III Road in the cul-de-sac and along the road. On the other side of the bay, Kaleiopapa Street has a small parking lot near the boat ramp. The Sheraton Kona Resort is perched on a cliff overlooking Keauhou Bay and accessible from Kaleiopapa Street. The Sheraton offers free guided tours of historical sites around Keauhou Bay. (Kona Sheraton Resort website)

Keauhou Bay with Sheraton Kona Resort above

9. Birthplace of King Kamehameha III

The birthplace of King Kamehameha III, is located up against the cliff on Keauhou Bay. The royal baby of King Kamehameha and his wife Keopuolani was born in 1813. He was named Kauikeaouli which means "placed in the dark clouds". At birth, he appeared to be stillborn, but the prophet Kapihe laid the baby on a rock, sprinkled him with water, and cooled him with a fan until he was revived. (Clark, 1985)

King Kamehameha III Birth Place at Keauhou Bay

Prince Kauikeaouli was given to Maui Chief Kaikioewa, then Governor of Kauai, to raise as was the custom at the time. At a young age Kauikeaouli became King when his older brother died of measles on his visit to London. During his reign he passed the first human rights act in 1839 and a Constitution in 1840. A legislature and cabinet replaced the council of chiefs and a court system was set up. The Great Mahele of 1848 gave land titles to chiefs and commoners and foreigners were allowed to own property for the first time. King Kamehameha III died in 1854 and was succeeded by his nephew, King Kamehameha IV. (Rhodes, 2001)

The Keauhou Shopping Center (78-6831 Alii Drive), at King Kamehameha III Road and Alii Drive, is owned by the Kamehameha Schools. A Heritage Center in the mall, next to the restrooms, has displays, photographs, and information about Hawaiian history and sites in the Keauhou area. The shopping center has a Farmer's Market every Saturday morning in the parking lot and regularly scheduled hula demonstrations and Hawaiian concerts. (Keauhou Village Shops website)

10. Kuamoo Battlefield

Lekeleke Burial Grounds from the Battle of Kuamoo

A lava field near Keauhou Bay was the location of a major battle in Hawaii that changed the direction of the new kingdom's history. In 1819, soon after the death of King Kamehameha, his widowed Queens and son Liholiho broke the ancient Kapu system which forbade women from eating with men and had the Hawaiian temples and idols destroyed. Kekuaokalani, Liholiho's cousin, opposed the end of the religion and led an army against Liholiho's royal army. Kekuaokalani and his wife Manono who fought by his side, were defeated at Battle of Kuamoo in December 1819 by the royal army led by Kalanimoku. (Ellis, 1827) Stacks of lava stones cover more than 300 fallen warriors on the lava battle field site called the Lekeleke Burial Grounds. A rock path leads along the lava field to the ocean cliffs.

There are no facilities at the site and parking is along the road. To get to the battlefield, drive south on Alii Drive, past Kaleiopapa Street (the road to the Sheraton). After the Keauhou Punahele condominiums, turn at the next right and follow the road to where it ends at the golf course. A plaque is on the left before the road dead ends.

HISTORIC SOUTH KONA TOUR

This South Kona driving tour describes historic sites on a coastal drive on Highway 160 from Kealakekua Bay to Honaunau Bay.

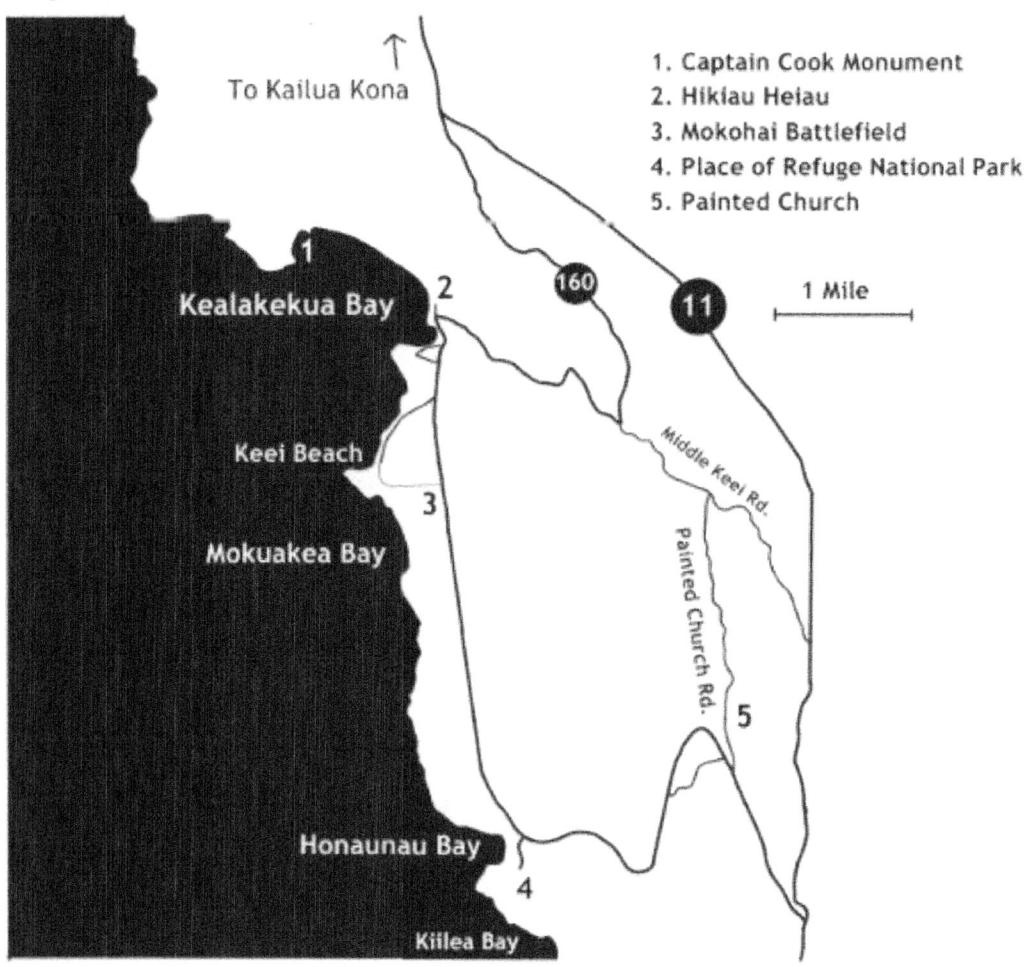

1. Captain Cook Monument
2. Hikiau Heiau
3. Mokohai Battlefield
4. Place of Refuge National Park
5. Painted Church

Map of Highway 160 in South Kona

The tour starts at the intersection of Highway 11 and Highway 160, 12 miles south of Palani Road in Kailua-Kona. The drive from

Kailua-Kona to the start of Highway 160 takes about 20 minutes or longer due to slow traffic and 20 to 35 mile speed limits. The Highway 160 turnoff is 1.6 miles past the McDonalds in South Kona on Highway 11. The start of Highway 160 is a 4.5 mile wiggly road down the cliff to Kealakekua Bay. At the bottom, turn right and drive past the Kealakekua Bay boat launch a short distance to a small parking lot next to the bay.

1. Captain Cook Monument

Kealakekua Bay with Captain Cook Monument barely visible

The Captain Cook Monument is a 27 foot white obelisk located on the north side of Kealakekua Bay. You can barely see the white monument in the distance across the bay from the parking lot. The monument was erected in 1874 at the location where the British explorer Captain Cook was killed in 1779. The site was later deeded to England in 1877. The only way to get close to the monument is on a guided kayak tour with a permitted commercial vendor, on a rented vessel with a valid permit, or by hiking the steep Kaawaloa trail.

Kealakekua means "pathway of the god" and the one-mile wide bay was once the site of major Hawaiian settlements.

When Captain Cook's ships, Resolution and Discovery, arrived in Hawaii he was welcomed as Lono, the god of agriculture and prosperity. Lono's emblem of an upright pole with crossbeam and tapa cloth looked like the masts and sails of the British ships. The story goes that Kamehameha first encountered Cook in 1778 on Maui where he was engaged in a battle in support of his uncle, King Kalaniopuu. Kamehameha investigated the strange ships that looked like floating temples with a crew that spoke gibberish, wore loose skin with holes (leather and pockets), had fire in their mouth (pipes), and made lightning and thunder from sticks (cannons). Cook left Maui for North America and returned to Hawaii in late 1778 for the warmer winter. (Desha, 2000)

Captain Cook's ships arrived in Kealakekua Bay on January 16th, 1779 during the winter festival of Makahiki which honors Lono with feasts and games. Thousands of Hawaiians were in the bay at the time to celebrate the festival and the priests treated Cook like a god, took him to Hikiau Heiau, and sacrificed animals in his honor. Cook was impressed with the Hawaiian's generosity and accepted their provisions, gifts, and entertainment. King Kalaniopuu offered part of his yearly tribute from the area, but the relationship started to become strained and Cook's ships finally left on February 4th. Unfortunately, they ran into bad weather and a foremast was destroyed so they had to return almost immediately. They arrived back in Kealakekua Bay on February 11th and found the bay deserted because the festival was over. The Hawaiians were persuaded to return to the area and help with repairs, however, hostilities broke out and Cook, four of his crew, and many Hawaiians were killed. (Ellis, 1827)

2. Hikiau Heiau

Walls of Hikiau Heiau next to Kealakekua Bay

Hikiau Heiau is the temple where Captain Cook was received as the god Lono on his arrival in Kealakekua Bay. A stone lava wall where the temple was located is next to the parking lot. Hikiau means "moving current" and the temple was built by King Kalaniopuu. Captain Cook performed the first Christian ceremony in Hawaii at this temple for a crew member who had died on January 28, 1779.

The missionary Ellis was curious about Captain Cook's death and was able to find people at Kaawaloa in 1823 who had witnessed the events 44 years earlier. The stories they told Ellis matched the reports from Cook's crew. The dispute was over a boat stolen from one of Cook's ships, probably for the metal nails. Cook planned to kidnap King Kalaniopuu and hold him on his ship until the boat was returned.

Unsuspecting, Kalaniopuu followed Cook to board his ship, however his wife Kalola had a bad feeling and begged him not to leave the shore. Suddenly, a warrior came running to them screaming about an attack. While Cook was on shore, one of his ships fired on a group of Hawaiian canoes and killed a chief. At this news the King sat down. Cook noticed the Hawaiians pick up stones and spears and he started towards his boat. A warrior hit him with a spear and he turned and shot him. Some accounts say Cook hit the King on the head to get him up. The King then struck Cook with a spear who fell and cried out from pain. Seeing that he was not a god, the Hawaiians started throwing stones at Cook and his men. His crew, watching from the ship, started firing on the Hawaiians. Cook turned toward the ships to tell them to stop, but the noise was too loud. With his back to the Hawaiians, he was stabbed and killed. Four other crew members with him were also killed that day on February 14, 1779. The day and night of battle that followed destroyed the village. After a truce, the crew was able to finish repairs and leave eight days later. Ellis believed that if Cook had remained facing the people they would not have killed him. (Ellis, 1827)

From the Kealakekua Bay parking lot, drive south past the Kealakekua Bay boat launch on the right. Continue south along the coast on Highway 160.

3. Mokuohai Battlefield

The tall grass and trees along the narrow Highway 160 makes it difficult to see the coastline and Keei beach. However, many historic events occurred along this 3 mile stretch of South Kona coastline.

Highway 160 near Mokuohai Battlefield

In 1782, on an unmarked lava field between Highway 160 and Mokuohai Bay, the Battle of Mokuohai was fought. This battle marked the beginning of Kamehameha's rise to power on Hawaii Island. Kamehameha, and a group of other chiefs, defeated King Kiwalao's army and he gained control of the west side of the island. The battle started a decade of bloody battles on Hawaii Island between rival chiefs until 1791 when Kamehameha killed his last rival and became King of Hawaii Island.

King Kalaniopuu distributed the districts of the island among his chiefs before he died in 1782. He gave his nephew Kamehameha custody of the war god Ku and his son Kiwalao rule of the island. However, the new King Kiwalao redistributed the land which angered the other chiefs. The power struggle resulted in the Battle of Mokuohai where Keeaumoku (the father of Kaahumanu and Kuakini and supporter of Kamehameha), killed the new King. During the battle, Keeaumoku got ahead of the other warriors and fell from stab wounds. His enemies thought he was dead. Kiwalao rushed up to snatch the highly prized whale tooth ornament around Keeaumoku's neck. When he leaned over Keeaumoku grabbed him by his long hair and pinned him down. When Kamehameha and his warriors caught up to Keeaumoku, they killed Kiwalao with their spears. The result of the battle split the island power with Kamehameha in the west, his rival Uncle Keawemauhili in Hilo, and his rival cousin Keoua

Kuahuula in Kau and Puna. In a strange twist of fate, the daughter of Kiwalao, Keopuolani, became Kamehameha's wife and mother of King Kamehameha II and III which made Kamehameha's rival cousin the grandfather of the Kamehameha dynasty. (Ellis, 1827)

4. Place of Refuge National Park

Royal Gardens next to Honaunau Bay

Puuhonua O Honaunau National Park is a picturesque and historic area on Honaunau Bay. A Puuhonua was a place of refuge where death from breaking a rule of the Kapu religion or losing in battle could be evaded. The Hawaiian Kapu religion usually punished those who broke the rules with death. At the Puuhonua, a Kahuna (priest) performed a ceremony which allowed the Kapu breaker to return home safely, often within hours. The Puuhonua was also used by the elderly, young, and defeated warriors to seek safety during the island's battles.

The 6-acre sanctuary is separated from the royal grounds by a massive rock wall. The royal grounds were off limits to commoners so those seeking refuge had to swim across Honaunau Bay or arrive by canoe. (Puuhonua O Honaunau National Park website)

Hale o Keawe (House of Keawe)

Kalanimoku was the Prime Minister during the early years of the Hawaii Kingdom. He was called the Iron Cable of Hawaii because of his abilities. As a young warrior he fought against Kamehameha during the 1782 Battle of Mokuohai. When Kalanimoku saw the young King Kiwalao and leader of the royal army killed, he ran 3 miles across the lava, with other surviving warriors, for protection at the Puuhonua at Honaunau Bay. The Hawaiian tradition of "forgiveness" and protection from death by the victors of battle, allowed Kalanimoku to survive and later become a prominent statesman in Hawaii. (Ellis, 1827)

The concept of forgiveness within the Kapu religion extended beyond specific places. Queen Kaahumanu was a Puuhonua with the authority to forgive Kapu breakers. (nps.gov)

The Visitor Center has a store, displays, and exhibits about the Puuhonua and royal grounds in the park. A one-half-mile, self-guided tour leads through the temples and sites along the bay in the national park. A two mile round trip trail leads to the remains of Kiilae Village. The park is open every day and charges a fee to enter. (Puuhonua O Honaunau National Park website)

Honaunau Bay and lava wall separating the Puuhonua

From the parking lot, turn right, away from the coast. The southern portion of Highway 160, from the national park up to Highway 11, is a wide and improved road. One mile from the parking lot is a scenic point where you can park and view Honaunau Bay and Kealakekua Bay from above.

To get to the painted church, turn left at Painted Church Road 2.6 miles from the national park entrance on Highway 160. The church's parking lot is on the right side 0.4 miles down the narrow, winding road.

5. St. Benedict's Painted Church

St. Benedict's Painted Church

St. Benedict's Painted Church (84-5140 Painted Church Road) is a small Catholic church that overlooks Honaunau Bay. The church is across a small bridge from the parking lot. Inside are colorful paintings of bible scenes.

The Painted Church was first located on Honaunau Bay near the Puuhonua. When the people began to move up to the more fertile land above the bay, Father John Berchmans Velghe from Belgium decided to move the church up the hill. The original St. Francis Regis chapel, built in 1842, was dismantled and moved in 1899. In 1902, the Bishop from Honolulu visited the church and renamed it for St. Benedict. Father

Velghe was a self-taught artist and painted the walls of the church with scenes from the bible in a gothic cathedral style. (Painted Church website)

Stations of the Cross are located above the parking lot on a grassy mountainside with a replica of Michelangelo's Pieta at the top.

Stations of the Cross at the Painted Church

From the intersection of Painted Church Road and Highway 160 it is 1.1 miles to Highway 11. Turn left on to Highway 11 to return to Kailua-Kona.

KONA COFFEE DRIVING EXPEDITION

Coffee Cherries hand sorted at Hula Daddy Coffee Farm

Kona coffee is grown on the slopes of Hualalai Volcano above Kailua-Kona. Hundreds of large and small Kona coffee farms are located along the Mamalahoa Highway from Holualoa to Kealakekua and many of the plantations are open to the public.

Reverend Samuel Ruggles brought the first coffee plants to Kona in 1828 and his plantings showed promise. In the 1840's coffee plantations thrived at altitudes of 800 to 1700 feet above sea level on the slopes of Mauna Loa and Hualalai in Kona. By the 1860's, most coffee plantations were abandoned because of a drop in coffee prices and patches of surviving coffee trees were harvested by the Hawaiians. The coffee boom of the 1890's brought coffee speculators back to Kona and thousands of acres were planted in just a few years. By 1905, the coffee boom had ended and only a few plantations survived. The land was divided into small farms and leased to Japanese sugar cane workers who managed the coffee plants through the ups and downs of the industry and produced world renown Kona coffee. (Goto, 1982)

This coffee excursion showcases only a few of the coffee plantations and gardens along Highway 180 in Holualoa and South

Kona. These coffee farms were selected because they are easy to access from the highway and have parking areas. They also have excellent coffee, friendly staff, and spectacular views of their coffee fields.

From Kailua-Kona, take Palani Road (Highway 190) to the intersection of Highway 180. This is the north end of Highway 180 (also called Mamalahoa Highway). Highway 180 winds down the slope with great views of Kailua Bay on clear days. The drive takes about 2 hours from Palani Road to Amy B.H. Greenwell Garden and back to Kailua-Kona on Highway 11 assuming short stops at each location. Verify times and dates on the coffee plantation's websites to make sure they are open and prepare for lots of delicious coffee samples.

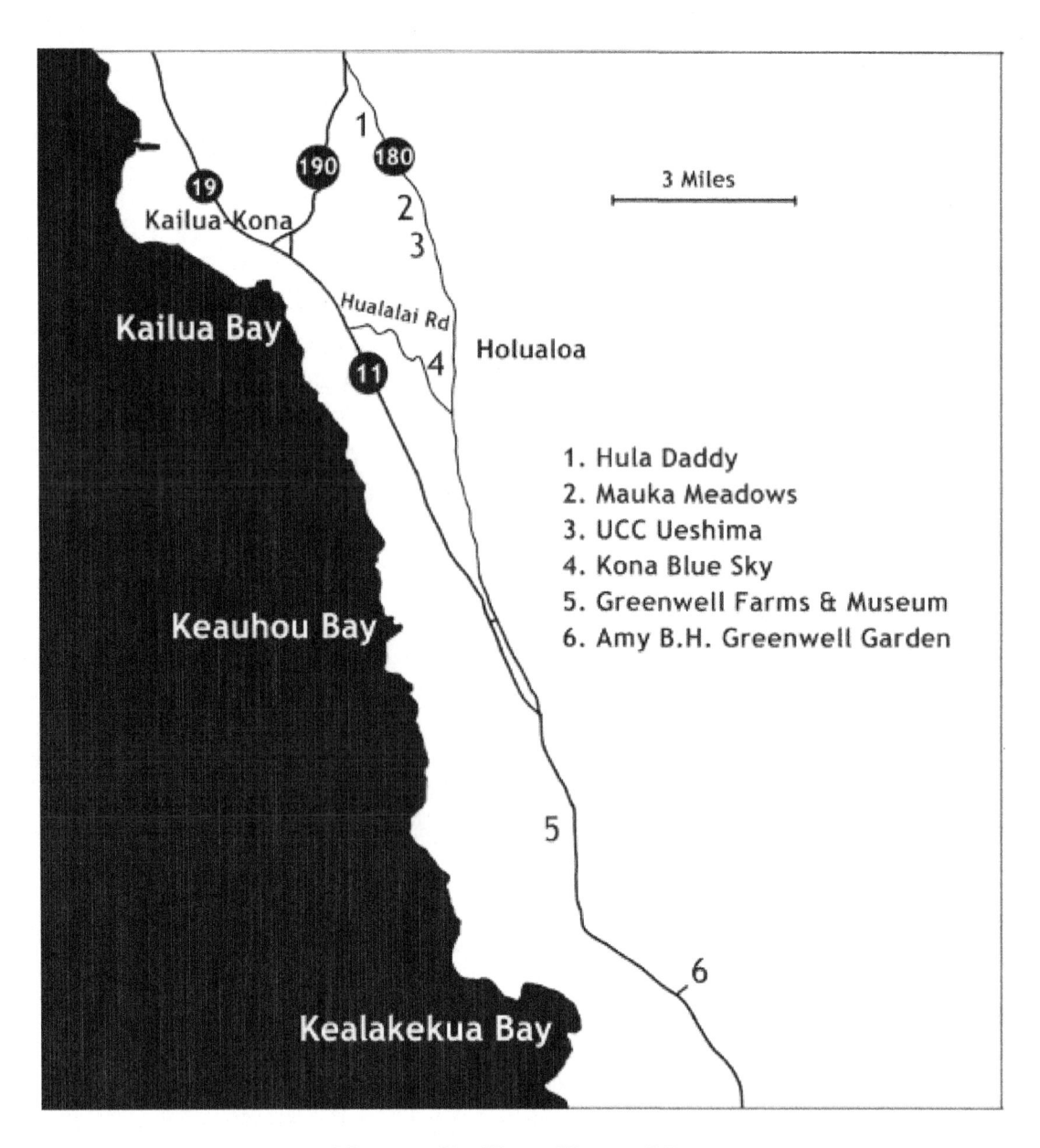

Kona Coffee Tour Map

1. Hula Daddy
2. Mauka Meadows
3. UCC Ueshima
4. Kona Blue Sky
5. Greenwell Farms & Museum
6. Amy B.H. Greenwell Garden

1. Hula Daddy Kona Coffee Farm

Hula Daddy Coffee Farm (74-4944 Mamalahoa Highway) has a parking area on the right side of the road, 0.7 miles from the north end of Highway 180. Inside is coffee tasting and a porch that overlooks the coffee fields and ocean below. During harvest season you can watch the coffee fruit being sorted and processed. Tours are available. (Hula Daddy Coffee Farm website)

Hula Daddy Coffee Visitor Center

2. Mauka Meadows Coffee Farm

Mauka Meadows Coffee Farm (75-5476 Mamalahoa Highway) has a parking area on the right side of the road, 3.3 miles from the north end of Highway 180. A self-guided tour starts at the parking area down a steep slope through colorful flowers, fruit gardens, and coffee fields.

Mauka Meadows is owned by a Japanese company called Doutor Coffee which specializes in coffee roasting and has coffee stores throughout Japan. Their coffee can be tasted and purchased next to the reflecting pool.

Mauka Meadows Coffee Farm

The tropical garden paths are marked with "Route" signs which lead to the reflecting pool at the bottom with a view of Kailua Bay.

Mauka Meadows flower gardens

Visitors are offered a ride up the steep hill to the parking lot from the coffee tasting area. This coffee plantation feels like a botanical garden and it is easy to spend hours enjoying and photographing the gardens and scenery. (Mauka Meadows website)

3. UCC Ueshima Kona Coffee Estate

UCC Ueshima is a Japanese coffee company that started as a store and is well known in Japan for their canned coffee drinks and coffee houses. Their coffee plantation in Hawaii (75-5568 Mamalahoa Highway) is located a half mile south on Highway 180 from Mauka Meadows. The parking lot is on the right side of the road next to a store that sells UCC coffee and snacks. Tours of the estate and special roasting tours are available by reservation. (UCC Hawaii website)

UCC Coffee fields behind their store

Holualoa village is located 5 miles from the north end of Highway 180. Along the road are art galleries, restaurants, coffee houses, churches, a theater, stores and the bright pink Kona Hotel. Every November during the Kona Coffee Festival, Holualoa has a village stroll of art galleries and dozens of coffee farms. (Holualoa Village website)

4. Kona Blue Sky Coffee Company

If you want to take a quick detour from Highway 180, turn right at the intersection of Hualalai Road, located 6 miles from the north end of Highway 180. The gate to Kona Blue Sky Coffee Company (76-973A Hualalai Road) is on the right side of the road 0.1 mile from the turn. The plantation has coffee tasting, information about coffee processing, and guided walking tours. (Kona Blue Sky Coffee website)

After returning to Highway 180, continue south past the Donkey Mill Art Center (Donkey Mill Art Center website) about 5 miles until it ends at Highway 11. Traffic is often congested in the South Kona corridor where Highway 180 intersects with Highway 11. Continue south on Highway 11 past the Aloha Theater, Mango Court, and other historic stores in the community of Kainaliu.

5. Greenwell Farms and Museum

Greenwell Coffee Farm sign on Highway 11

Greenwell Farms (81-6581 Mamalahoa Highway) is located 2.5 miles south of the junction of Highway 180 and Highway 11 on the right side of the road. From the parking lot on Highway 11, drive back to the Greenwell Farms Visitor Center to a store and coffee tasting area. It is open Monday through Sunday and tours of the coffee fields and processing facilities are available. (Greenwell Farms website)

Henry Greenwell came to Hawaii from England in 1850 and spent 40 years farming and ranching in Kona. Greenwell took great care in selecting his coffee for the international market and when Kona's coffee industry declined in the late 1860's, H. N. Greenwell coffee retained its high quality and his trademark gained acclaim. In 1873, Greenwell's coffee was given an award at the World's Fair in Vienna, Austria and he is credited with starting "Kona Coffee". His 36,000 acres were passed down to his 10 children. His great grandson now owns Greenwell Farms. (Goto, 1982) (Greenwell Farms website)

Greenwell Visitor Center display

The Kona Historical Society has a museum in Greenwell's Store next to Greenwell Farms. They charge an entrance fee when the museum is open on Monday and Thursday.

Henry Greenwell Store Museum

On Thursdays, a Portuguese stone oven next to Greenwell's Store is used to cook fresh bread. The Kona Historical Society also operates a living coffee museum across from Amy B.H. Greenwell Ethnobotanical Garden. (Kona Historical Society website)

6. Amy BH Greenwell Ethnobotanical Garden

Amy Greenwell Ethnobotanical Visitor's Center

Amy B. H. Greenwell Ethnobotanical Garden (82-6160 Mamalahoa Highway) is a 15 acre garden with over 200 native Hawaiian and Polynesian plant species. The landscape has four climatic zones with indigenous and Polynesian plants specific to them. There are stonework features of the Kona Field System introduced by King Umi within the garden. A path through the garden has markers describing every plant and their uses.

The garden is open Tuesday to Sunday and closed on Mondays and holidays. There is a fee to enter and guided plant tours are offered daily. (Bishop Museum's Greenwell Park website)

Amy Greenwell inherited a small portion of her grandfather Henry Greenwell's 36,000 acres in Kona. Amy graduated from Stanford University in 1942 and later returned to Hawaii to work with the Bishop Museum on its archeological projects. She transformed her 15 acre property into a garden with only native and Polynesian plants and left her property to the Bishop Museum when she died in 1974. (bishopmuseum.org/greenwell/amygreenwell.html)

Events and Festivals in Kona

Annual Festivals in Kona

Iolani Luahine Hula Festival (January)
Grow Hawaiian Festival (February)
Kona Brewers Festival (March)
Kona Orchid Show (May)
Kailua-Kona Kamehameha Parade (June)
Puuhonua o Honaunau Park Cultural Festival (June)
Kona Marathon (June)
Kailua-Kona Independence Day Parade (July)
Kona International Billfish Tournament (August)
Mai Tai Festival (August)
Slack Key Guitar Festival (September)
Liliuokalani Long Distance Canoe Races (September)
Kupuna Hula Festival (September)
Ironman World Championships (October)
Kona Coffee Cultural Festival (November)
Holuloa Village Coffee and Art Stroll (November)
Arbor Day at Amy Greenwell Garden (November)
Kailua-Kona Christmas Parade (December)
Holualoa Music and Light Festival (December)

Performers on Alii Drive during Kailua-Kona Village Stroll

Regular Events and Activities in Kona
Aloha Theater
Astronaut Ellison Onizuka Space Center (Keahole Airport)
Donkey Mill Art Center in Holualoa
Kailua-Kona Village Stroll
KBXtreme bowling and arcade
Kona Book Club
Kona Commons
Kona Historical Society
Kona Outdoor Circle

CHAPTER 2: KOHALA RESORTS AND BEACHES

Mauna Lani Bay Hotel

The western coastline of South Kohala, has a dry, sunny climate with white sand beaches and turquoise-blue ocean bays. Most of the island's resorts are located in the district of South Kohala, which is located north of Kona, to take advantage of its weather and beaches. This chapter describes resort beaches and historical sites in the area.

1. Mauna Kea Beach
2. Hapuna Beach State Park
3. Puako Beach 69
4. Holoholokai Beach and Petroglyphs
5. Kalahuipuaa Trail
6. The 49 Black Sand Beach
7. A Bay and Royal Fish Ponds
8. Kings Trail and Petroglyphs

A. Mauna Kea Beach Hotel
B. Hapuna Beach Prince Hotel
C. Fairmont Orchid
D. Mauna Lani Bay Hotel
E. Shops at Mauna Lani
F. Hilton Waikoloa Village
G. Waikoloa Beach Marriott
H. Kings Shops
I. Queen's Marketplace
J. Helipad (Blue Hawaiian)
K. Waikoloa Village Market

Map of South Kohala Sites, Resorts and Shopping Areas

1. Mauna Kea Beach

Mauna Kea Beach

　　Mauna Kea Beach, also known as Kaunaoa Beach, is located within the Mauna Kea Resort in front of the Mauna Kea Beach Hotel. The crescent-shaped bay has pristine white sand with a gradual slope into the ocean.

　　The beach is open to the public, but there are only 30 public parking spaces. The limited access to the beach makes it less crowded than nearby Hapuna Beach. Rocks at the south end of the bay are the best area to snorkel when the water is calm. There are no lifeguards. The beach has restrooms and showers.

　　The entrance to the beach is 25 miles north of Keahole Airport Road near mile marker 68. From Highway 19 (Queen Kaahumanu Highway) turn toward the ocean on to Mauna Kea Beach Drive. At the gate, the guards will provide a parking pass and directions to the public beach parking area if spaces are available. From the parking area, it is a 5 minute walk down to the beach. (Mauna Kea Beach Hotel website)

Granite Buddha from India at Mauna Kea Beach Hotel

In the 1960's Lawrence Rockefeller got a lease on the land around Kaunaoa Bay from Richard Smart, the owner of Parker Ranch in Waimea. Rockefeller built the Mauna Kea Beach Hotel which opened in 1965 and was the first luxury hotel on an outer island at the time. The hotel has 1,600 pieces of Asian and Pacific Island art on display. In 1994 another hotel opened in the Mauna Kea resort complex, the Hapuna Beach Prince Hotel. (Hapuna Beach Prince Hotel website)

The entrance to the Hapuna Beach Prince Hotel is accessible on Kaunaoa Drive which is on the opposite of side of Highway 19 from the Mauna Kea Hotel entrance. There is no public parking for Hapuna Beach at the Hapuna Beach Prince Hotel. Hapuna Beach is accessible by a road just south of the Mauna Kea Resort.

2. Hapuna Beach State Park

Hapuna Beach is one of the most popular beaches on the island for residents and visitors and usually crowded on holidays and weekends. The half-mile long, white sand beach is crescent shaped with clear, aquamarine colored water and a gentle slope of soft sand into the ocean.

Hapuna Beach

During the winter months, Hapuna Beach has big waves which are good for boogie boarding and body surfing. The beach has lifeguards who post warnings if there are any dangers and provide information on how to stay safe.

Walking path to Hapuna Beach

Hapuna Beach State Park entrance is 24 miles north of Keahole Airport Road on Highway 19. From Highway 19 turn toward the ocean on Hapuna Beach Road and follow it 0.4 miles to the parking lot. There is a parking fee for non-residents. The beach is easy to walk to on a paved path from the parking lot and there is a loading zone to drop off passengers and heavy items close to the beach. The park has well maintained facilities with restrooms, showers, and picnic areas.

South of Hapuna Beach State Park is Puako, a small neighborhood along the coastal road, Puako Beach Drive.

3. Puako Beach 69

Beach 69 in Puako

Beach 69 in Puako, also known as Waialea Beach, was named for its location near mile marker 69 on Highway 19. The beach is popular because of the trees that provide shade and create private little coves.

To get to Beach 69, turn on to Puako Beach Drive toward the ocean from Highway 19 between mile marker 70 and 71. Turn right at the first intersection, across from the county garbage facility, onto the single lane Old Puako Road. The road leads to a parking lot on the left. The beach has restrooms, showers, and picnic tables. There are no lifeguards.

The Mauna Lani Resort is south of Puako, accessible from Highway 19 between mile markers 74 and 73. The resort has two hotels, the Fairmont Orchid and Mauna Lani Bay Hotel, vacation condominiums, golf courses, ancient Hawaiian fishponds, and white sand beaches.

4. Holoholokai Beach and Puako Petroglyph Reserve

Holoholokai Beach Park has a rocky beach that is not safe for swimming. The park has picnic tables, restrooms, and a parking lot. The trailhead to the Puako Petroglyph Reserve is next to the parking lot.

Holoholokai Beach Park in Mauna Lani Resort

To get to the park, turn on to Mauna Lani Drive from Highway 19, located 19.4 miles north of Keahole Airport Road. Mauna Lani Drive leads to a circular intersection; take the first right on to North Kaniku Drive before the Shops at Mauna Lani. Turn right before the Fairmont Hotel entrance onto Holoholokai Beach Park Road and drive to the parking lot.

A paved path to the Puako Petroglyph Reserve starts in the parking lot. A sidewalk leads to an area where samples of the petroglyphs are displayed and rubbings can be taken. From there, a 0.7 mile rough lava trail winds through a forest of kiawe (mesquite) trees to a viewing platform that surrounds the petroglyphs. There are over 3000 images believed to have been carved into the lava between 1000 and 1800 AD. Some of the carved drawings are of figures and one group of 30 figures resembles a column of warriors.

The carved images are easiest to see in the morning or late afternoon light.

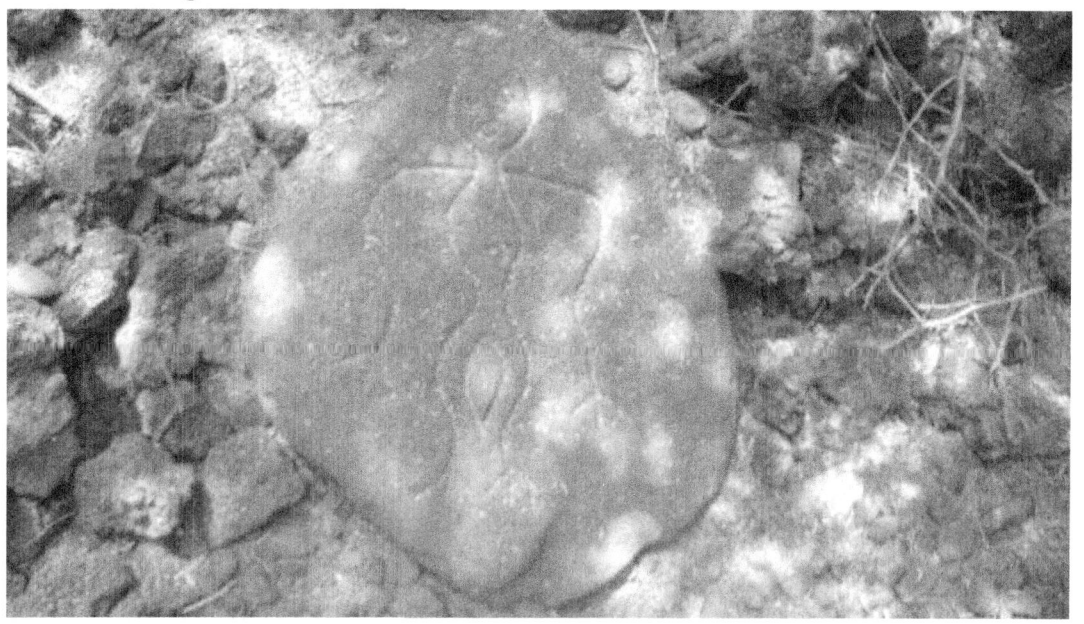

Petroglyph replica at Puako Petroglyph Preserve

The Fairmont Orchid is on 32 acres of oceanfront property within the 3,200-acre Mauna Lani Resort. The hotel opened in December 1990 as a Ritz Carlton and was later managed by Starwood Hotels Resorts as The Orchid at Mauna Lani. Since December 2003 the property has been managed by Fairmont Hotels Resorts. (Fairmont Orchid website)

The historic Kalahuipuaa area in Mauna Lani Resort has a public parking lot on Pauoa Road. From the circular intersection turn on to Mauna Lani Drive next to the Shops at Mauna Lani. Turn left on to Pauoa Road before the Mauna Lani Bay Hotel entrance. The public parking lot is on the right near the Mauna Lani Sports and Fitness Club.

5. Kalahuipuaa Trail and Fish pond in Mauna Lani

    The Kalahuipuaa Trail starts next to the public parking lot on Pauoa Road. The paved trail crosses a lava field to ancient Hawaiian fishponds and beautiful white sand beaches. Markers on the trail point out a lava tube shelter cave, tool making area, and petroglyphs. The trail leads to a brackish (salt and fresh water) lagoon with seven ancient fish ponds that were used to raise fish for Hawaiian royalty. The largest fish pond called Kalahuipuaa, which means "family of pigs", is 4.6 acres in size.

Public Parking lot at Kalahuipuaa Trail in Mauna Lani

    The paved trail loops around the fish ponds lined with coconut, noni, breadfruit, and other native trees. The fishponds closest to the coast have sluice gates that let fresh seawater and small fish in from the ocean. Awa (milkfish) and amaama (mullet) are still raised in the well maintained ponds.

Path along Kalahuipuaa fishpond in Mauna Lani Resort

At the end of the trail is a white sand beach just south of the Mauna Lani Bay Hotel. Kamehameha had a canoe landing next to the fishponds and a replica of a canoe house is on the beach. Haleakala Volcano on Maui Island is often visible across the channel. During the winter whales can be seen breaching. A walkway across the Waipuhi fish pond retaining wall leads to the Mauna Lani Bay Hotel.

South of the beach with the canoe house is a grassy area with the Eva Parker Woods Cottage Museum. Next to the lanai of the cottage is a walkway across the retaining wall between the largest fishpond and the ocean. It leads to a white sand beach in a protected cove in front of the Mauna Lani Beach Club. When the restaurant Napua in the clubhouse is open, drinks and meals can be purchased. Lifeguards are employed by the resort and restrooms are located in the clubhouse.

The Mauna Lani Bay Resort has a program to foster Hawaiian turtles called honu. The turtles are raised in salt water ponds within the hotel lobby and outside until they are large enough to be released. Every 4th of July, the resort has a release ceremony for the mature turtles. The turtles do not venture far away and can often be seen sunning on the beach along the shoreline within the Mauna Lani Resort. (Mauna Lani Bay Hotel website)

Turtle sunning on beach in Mauna Lani Resort

Francis Hyde Ii Brown was a state senator for 20 years and known as "Mr. Golf". Brown bought the Kalahuipuaa fishponds and the Eva Parker Woods Cottage in the 1930's. He met Noboru Gotoh, chairman of the Tokyu Corporation, at the 1964 Olympics in Tokyo. They became friends and planned to build a resort at Kalahuipuaa around the fishponds with a golf course. They named the resort Mauna Lani (meaning mountains reaching heaven) in honor of the five volcanoes which can be seen from within the resort (Mauna Kea, Mauna Loa, Kohala, Hualalai, and Haleakela on Maui). Francis Brown died in 1976 before construction began on Mauna Lani Bay Hotel, which opened in 1983. The resort's two championship golf courses are named Francis Brown North and South. (maunalani.com/press/fact-sheet-kalahuipuaa-at-mauna-lani)

To get to the Kalahuipuaa Trail parking lot, turn on to Mauna Lani Drive from Highway 19 and at the circular intersection take the second right turn to continue on Mauna Lani Drive toward the coast. Turn left on to Pauoa Road and the public parking lot is down the road on the right side. Restrooms are located in the parking lot.

6. 49 Black Sand Beach in Mauna Lani Resort

Honokaope Bay in Mauna Lani Resort

The 49 Black Sand Beach on Honokaope Bay is within the Mauna Lani Resort. The small beach has lava rock cliffs and a shoreline fisherman trail in a gated community within Mauna Lani. The bay is popular for snorkeling. There are no lifeguards.

Access to the beach is through a gatehouse on Honokaope Place. To get to the beach, turn onto Mauna Lani Drive from Highway 19 and at the circular intersection, take the third right turn onto South Kaniku Drive. Turn left at Honokaope Place and stop at the gate. There is limited parking at the end of Honokaope Place on the left side of the road. Cross the road to walk down to the beach.

The Waikoloa Beach Resort is south of Mauna Lani, accessible from Highway 19 on Waikoloa Beach Road. The complex has the

Marriott and Hilton resorts, vacation condominiums, golf courses, ancient fishponds, and a white sand beach.

7. Anaehoomalu Bay in Waikoloa Beach Resort

Anaehoomalu Bay (often shortened to A-Bay) is a white sand beach with a grove of coconut trees. The bay is a popular place to swim, snorkel, and windsurf.

Anaehoomalu Bay in Waikoloa Beach Resort

The Waikoloa Beach Marriott Resort faces Anaehoomalu Bay behind two ancient Hawaiian fishponds. (Waikoloa Marriott Resort website) A large public parking area is located at the southern end of the Anaehoomalu Bay with picnic tables, showers, and restrooms.

Waikoloa Beach is 17 miles north of Keahole Airport Road on Highway 19. At the traffic light, turn toward the coast on Waikoloa Beach Drive. Turn left at Kuualii Place, past the Queen's Shops, and drive to the parking lot. A restaurant called the Lava Lava Beach Club is located on the beach.

Paved Path through Royal Fishponds at Waikoloa Marriott Hotel

Anaehoomalu means "protected mullet" referring to the mullet fish raised in the Waikoloa fish ponds. A paved path between the Marriott Resort and the beach circles the fishponds. A restored Hawaiian village with the rock foundations of houses and shrines is located on the path with informative signs.

Across Waikoloa Beach Drive from the Marriott Resort is an ancient Hawaiian site with petroglyphs in the middle of the Waikoloa golf course.

8. Waikoloa Beach Petroglyphs and Kings Trail

Petroglyphs at Waikoloa

Waikoloa Petroglyph Preserve is located on the King's Trail in Waikoloa Beach Resort. The most common carvings are dots, holes, and circles which have various interpretations including representations for journeys made and indications of children born. The area has hundreds of carvings of human figures, turtles, crabs, canoes, and fishhooks. The age of the earliest carvings are estimated to be 800 AD when the area was first settled. Some unusual carvings include a Hawaiian cowboy, a surfer, and a church. (James, 1995)

Kings Trail in Waikoloa Beach

Stone walls, used as wind breakers by travelers on the road, can also be seen next to the Kings Trail where most of the petroglyphs are located.

> *The Kings Trail (Ala Kahakai) was improved by King Kalakaua in the 1870's to drive cattle through the rough lava fields from the ranches to the ships. It was built over ancient trails to be straight and level with curbs of stone to guide the cattle. Prisoners and tax debtors were used to build the road. (nps.gov/alka)*

The Kings Trail and petroglyphs can be reached from the Kings Shops parking lot on Waikoloa Beach Drive. Portions of the Kings Trail are very difficult to walk on, but it can be bypassed by walking on the golf cart trail along the Kings Trail to an entrance near the petroglyphs. Mornings are the best time to see the lava carvings and the coolest time of day.

Hilton Waikoloa Village Resort art walk

    The Hilton Waikoloa Village Resort is like a mini-amusement park with fantastic views and walking areas. The Hilton resort has tropical gardens, waterfalls, exotic wildlife, dolphin tank, lagoon, and an art walk with 1800 Asian and Polynesian pieces on display. The resort has a train, canal boat, and garden paths through the 62 acre property. The hotel charges for parking. (Waikoloa Hilton Resort website)

Events and Festivals near the Kohala Resorts
Annual Festivals at Kohala Resorts

Ocean Film Festival (January)
Ukulele Festival (March)
Big Island Chocolate Festival at the Fairmont (March)
Lavaman Waikoloa Triathlon (March)
Big Island Film Festival at Mauna Lani (May)
Jazz and Blues Festival at Mauna Kea Beach (May)
Waikoloa Rubber Duckie Race and Fireworks (July 4)
Turtle Independence Day at Mauna Lani (July 4)
Great Waikoloa Canoe Race (August)
Floating Lantern Ceremony at the Fairmont (August)
Festival of Aloha at Hapuna Beach Prince (October)
Christmas at the Fairmont (December)
Annual Poke Contest Waikoloa (September)
Falsetto and Storytelling contest Waikoloa (September)
Taste of Hawaiian Range and Ag Festival (October)
Annual Moku O Keawe Hula Festival (November)

Dolphin Quest at the Waikoloa Hilton

Regular Events and Activities near Kohala Events
Dolphin Quest at Hilton hotel
Shops at Mauna Lani events
Queen's Marketplace and King's Shops events and Farmers Market
Helicopter tours from Waikoloa
Game Hunting on Parker Ranch
Cowboy adventures at Kahua Ranch and Ponoholo Ranch

CHAPTER 3: HILO

Hilo across the Bay from Liliuokalani Garden

Hilo, on the east side of Hawaii Island, has a warm and wet climate, tropical gardens, green parks, and a blend of Hawaiian and Asian cultures. The town is the county seat with a University of Hawaii campus, community college, and international astronomy centers. Hilo has a bustling downtown, malls, harbor, airport, and the largest population on the island

The maps and tours in this chapter have unique and beautiful places with information to drive and sightsee in and near Hilo. The Hilo Driving Tour has some special sites that showcase the town's beauty, history, and delicious foods. The Downtown Hilo Walking Tour provides a guide to museums, parks, and historical sites along the Wailuku River. A map and descriptions of Hilo area beaches and gardens are also included.

HILO DRIVING TOUR

This section has a guided drive of the town's tropical gardens, waterfalls, parks, and historic sites. The places on the tour can be seen from a car window or a short walk from the parking lot.

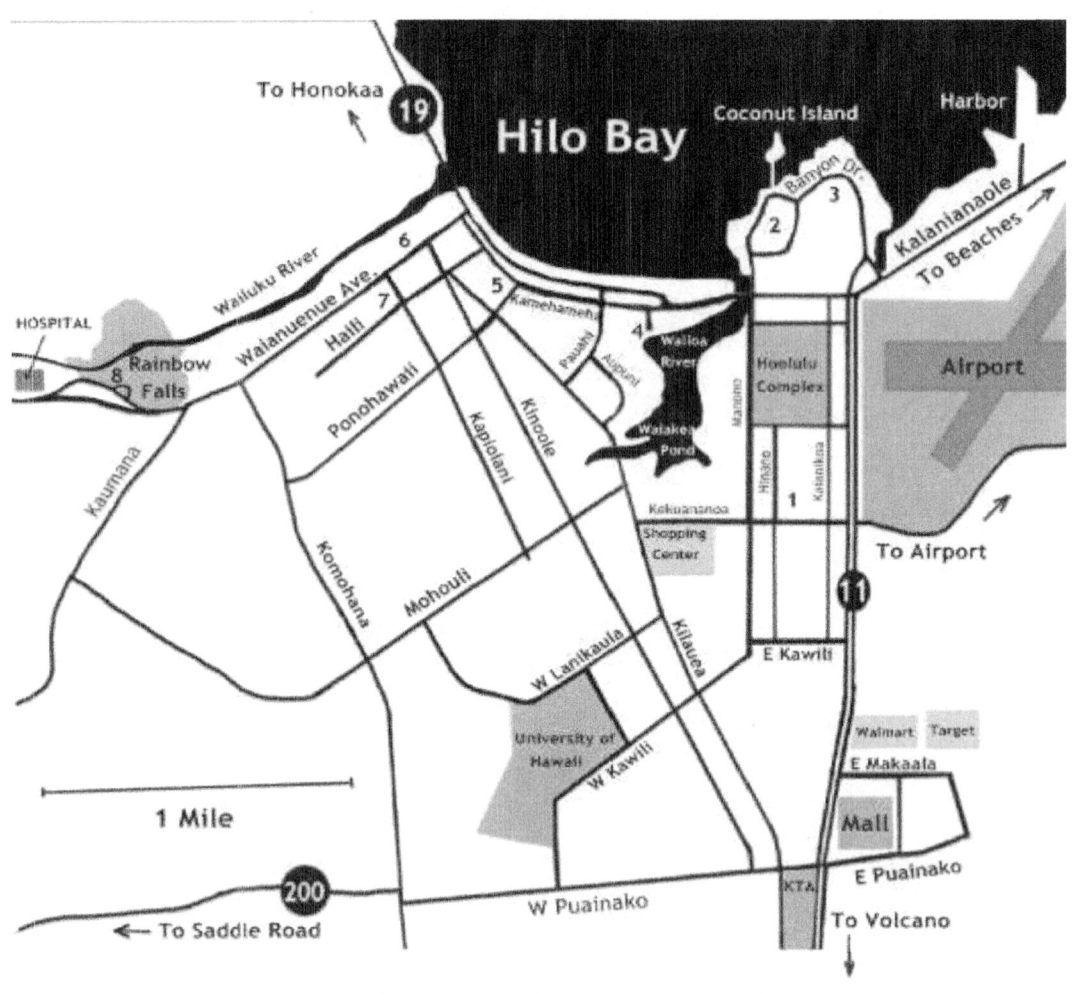

1. Big Island Candies Factory
2. Liliuokalani Gardens/Coconut Island
3. Banyon tree walk/Reeds Bay
4. King Kamehameha statue
5. Farmer's Market and downtown
6. Naha and Pinao Stones/Hilo Public Library
7. Lyman Museum and Mission House
8. Rainbow Falls and Wailuku River

Hilo Town and Driving Tour Map

1. Big Island Candies

    Big Island Candies (585 Hinano Street) offers Hawaiian-themed chocolates and cookies that are delightfully wrapped. Visitors are offered samples of cookies, chocolates, and Kona coffee. The factory floor where workers are making chocolates and cookies can be seen through a glass wall. Cookies, candies, and ice cream are sold in the store which is open every day. (Big Island Candies website)

Big Island Candies factory

    From Highway 11, turn onto Kekuanaoa Street, the opposite direction of the Hilo airport entrance (it is a left turn when coming from Volcano). Turn right on Hinano Street (the 3rd street from Highway 11 on Kekuanaoa Street).

The company was started in 1977 by a Hilo couple who have had great success at creating delicious Hawaiian products with a global appeal. The store is often bustling with bus loads of Japanese visitors buying *"omiyage"* (gifts to take home).

"Omiyage" is a gift purchased on a trip for family, friends, and coworkers. The Japanese custom requires that a specialty product from the places visited, usually food, be brought home. Omiyage is expected to be attractive and beautifully wrapped. Hawaii has adopted the omiyage custom of bringing something homemade to gatherings of friends or family.

From Big Island Candies parking lot turn left on to Hinano Street and right on to Kekuanaoa Street. Then take the next right at Manono Street. Manono Street passes by Hilo's Civic Auditorium which is in Hoolulu Park.

Hoolulu Park is a square block of county facilities which includes Afook-Chinen Civic Auditorium, Walter Victor Baseball Complex, Dr. Francis F.C. Wong Stadium, Kawamoto Swim Stadium, and Edith Kanakaole Multi-Purpose Stadium where the annual Merrie Monarch Hula Festival is held.

At the intersection of Manono and Kamehameha Avenue (Highway 19) go straight across on to Banyan Drive (also called Lihiwai Street). Suisan Fish Store is on the left and Liliuokalani Garden is directly ahead. Liliuokalani Garden's parking lot is at the other end of the park. Drive around the park and turn left on Lihiwai Street, a one-way road into the parking area.

2. Liliuokalani Garden and Coconut Island

Bridge in Liliuokalani Garden

    Liliuokalani Garden is the largest Edo-style Japanese garden outside of Japan and is centered around Waihonu Pond with bridges, pagodas, and stone lanterns lining paved walking paths. The 30 acre garden was originally dedicated in 1917 and named for the last monarch in Hawaii. The garden paths wind through flowering trees, bamboo glades, and acres of lush and manicured grass with views of Hilo Bay. From the parking lot, downtown Hilo is visible across the bay below Mauna Kea Volcano. The garden has benches to sit and enjoy the views and restrooms are a short walk from the parking area.

Two major tsunamis destroyed Liliuokalani Garden in 1946 and 1960. In 1968, the garden was rebuilt to commemorate the 100th anniversary of the arrival of first Japanese immigrants to work in the sugar cane fields. Stone lions and lanterns were donated by towns in Japan and in 1997 a tea ceremony house was given to the park by Dr. Soshitsu Zen, a grand tea master.

Coconut Island across a footbridge in Hilo Bay

Coconut Island (also called Moku Ola) is in Hilo Bay near Liliuokalani Garden. The footbridge to the island is near the Liliuokalani Garden parking lot and a smaller parking lot is located closer to the island next to the Hilo Hawaiian Hotel.

Moku Ola means island of life and health. According to legend, the island has curative spring waters and people who swim around one of the rocks at the eastern inlet will recover from their illness. The island was a place of refuge (Puuhonua) where Hawaiians were safe from punishment, which was usually death, when they broke one of the Kapu laws. There was a luakini type heiau (temple where human sacrifice took place) named Makaoku across the channel from Coconut Island. It was a pyramid of stone 30 feet high. The stones were removed from the site in 1860 by Captain Thomas Spencer to build a boat landing at the mouth of the Wailoa River. (Thrum, 1907)

World War II Tower on Coconut Island

Coconut Island's protected coves are popular with families and a concrete diving tower, used to train pilots during World War II, is a favorite place for jumping into the bay. The island has covered picnic areas, restrooms, and showers.

The Suisan Fish Market is located near the intersection of Banyan Drive and Kamehameha Avenue (Highway 19), a short walk from the Liliuokalani Garden parking lot. The retail store was started by Japanese fishermen in 1907 and the company has grown into a major distributor of fish and other foods to restaurants and grocery stores. Their location, on Sampan boat harbor, was their first and had to be rebuilt twice after being destroyed by tsunamis. (Suisan fish company website)

Depending on the season, the fish market has Ahi (tuna), Mahi Mahi (dolphin fish), and Ono (Wahoo). There are buckets full of colorful reef fish that many visitors are surprised people eat. Suisan also sells "poke" (a favorite food in Hawaii made from cubes of raw fish and spices) and other snacks. A takeout grill is located outside the building.

Suisan Fish Market and dock on Sanpan boat harbor

Behind the Suisan Fish Market building is a Rakuen (Happiness) Garden constructed by Kazuo Nakamura, a landscape architect from Kyoto. The garden is dedicated to the senior citizens on Hawaii Island and overlooks the Wailoa River and Hilo Bay.

Hilo Rakuen Garden

From Liliuokalani Garden's parking lot, turn left on to Banyan Drive. Drive past Liliuokalani Garden on the left and under the Banyan trees where Hilo's major hotels are located on the bay. The parking lot for Reed's Bay is located on the left.

3. <u>Banyan tree walk and Reeds Bay</u>
Banyan Drive circles Waiakea Peninsula on Hilo Bay under a thick canopy of old Banyan trees. The Banyan trees along the road are "named trees" with wooden signs to identify the famous person

who planted it. The most popular tree on Banyan Drive was planted by George Herman, "Babe Ruth" in 1933.

The idea of celebrities planting tree saplings started in 1933, the year Cecil DeMille was in Hilo filming "Four Frightened People". DeMille, his wife, and several actors planted trees. In 1934 President Franklin Roosevelt planted a tree and the crushed coral road was replaced with a paved road through the trees. Trees have been planted over the years by authors, religious leaders, politicians, adventurers, movie stars, and local Hawaiians. The tsunamis in 1946 and 1960 destroyed some of the trees, but many survived and still thrive today. (Hilo Bayfront Trails Master Plan, County of Hawaii, 2009)

Famous trees on Banyan Drive

Restaurants and coffee shops with views of Hilo Bay are located in the Hilo Hawaiian Hotel (website), Uncle Billy's Hilo Bay

Hotel (website), Naniloa Volcanoes Hotel (website) and other hotels and condominiums on Banyan Drive along the sidewalk to Reed's Bay.

Reeds Bay on Banyan Drive

Reed's Bay is a shallow bay used to anchor sail boats and has a protected area for swimming. Across Reed's Bay, cruise ships and container ships can often be seen docked at Hilo Harbor. Reed's Bay has restrooms next to the parking lot.

Hilo Ice Pond

Next to Reed's Bay is the "ice pond" which is a popular place to swim during the hot summer months. The pond is very cold because of natural springs that produce fresh water that rises above the salt water. The pond extends to Kalanianaole Avenue where a restaurant sits next to it and is across from the Hilo Seaside Hotel.

Continue on Banyan Drive past Reed's Bay to the Kamehameha Avenue intersection. Turn right and the Naniloa Country Club Golf Course is on the right past some warehouses. The Waiakea Tsunami Clock, which stopped when the *tsunami* struck at 1:05 A.M. on May 23, 1960, is on the right side of the road next to the golf course. Drive over the Wailoa River bridge and take a left turn 0.4 miles from the bridge into Wailoa River State Park. At the end of the road is a parking area next to the King Kamehameha Statue.

4. Kamehameha Statue and Wailoa River Park

King Kamehameha statue facing Hilo Bay

The 14 foot bronze statue of King Kamehameha is a replica of the original statue made in Italy (the original statue is in Kapaau in North Kohala on the Big Island). The statue is surrounded by the 130 acre Wailoa River State Park. This green expanse was once a town called Shinmachi, "New Town", which was destroyed by a tsunami in 1946 and again in 1960. A memorial plaque for Shinmachi is in the parking lot, to the left when facing the King Kamehameha statue. More about Shinmachi and the tsunami devastation of Hilo can be found at the Pacific Tsunami Museum in downtown Hilo. Waiakea pond and the unusual hump shaped footbridges across the Wailoa River can be seen from the statue parking area.

When the missionary William Ellis visited Hilo in 1823, the main settlements were on the Wailoa River and Waiakea peninsula in Hilo Bay. The Waiolama stream flowed into fish ponds and irrigated the crops planted in the area. Hilo had a wide, crescent-shaped, black sand beach that extended from the mouth of the Wailoa River to the Wailuku River. The long waves into Hilo Bay were considered the best surfing in Hawaii. (Ellis, 1827)

The sugar cane boom in Hilo in the early 1900's increased traffic between Hilo and ships anchored at the mouth of the Wailoa River. During heavy rains the Waiolama stream washed out the road to Hilo. Starting in 1915, sand from Hilo Bay's beach was used for landfill to divert the Waiolama into the Wailoa River. Over the next 8 years, Hilo Bay's beach was reduced to a narrow strip. In 1929, the completed Hilo Bay breakwater killed the reef in the bay and blocked the surfing waves. (Kelly, 1981) (Clark, 1985)

Hump bridges over Wailoa River

Return to Kamehameha Avenue and turn left towards downtown Hilo. At the intersection of Kamehameha and Pauahi Streets, continue straight ahead. Hilo Farmer's Market is on the left just past the Shell station.

5. Farmer's Market and Downtown Hilo

Hilo's Farmers Market (400 Kamehameha Avenue) is on the corner of Kamehameha Avenue and Mamo Street. The market was started in 1988 with only four farmers and has grown to more than two hundred vendors. Hilo's Farmers Market has been featured in travel and cooking magazines for its exceptional selection of tropical island fruits, vegetables, and flowers. The Downtown Hilo Walking Tour, in the next section, has more information about the Farmer's Market, historic places in downtown Hilo, and nearby parking areas.

Open Air Farmer's Market in downtown Hilo

Continue on Kamehameha Avenue to the intersection at Waianuenue Avenue. Turn left on Waianuenue Avenue and drive past the Federal Building on the right, Kalakaua Park on the left to Hilo Public Library on the right side of the road.

6. Naha Stone and Hilo Public Library

Two huge stones sit in front of the Hilo Public Library on Waianuenue Avenue between Ululani and Kapiolani Streets. The large stone is the Naha stone, which became famous after Kamehameha flipped the massive stone and predicted his destiny of becoming the first King to unite all the islands of Hawaii. The smaller stone is called Pinao which is said to have been part of an ancient temple called Kaipalaoa located near the Hilo Armory. (Thrum, 1907)

According to legend, the 3.5 ton Naha stone was brought from Kauai Island in a canoe in the 12th century. The royal birthstone was the mark of the Naha chiefs. When a Naha chiefess had a son, the child was placed on the stone and a priest offered a prayer to the gods. If the child did not cry until the prayer was completed, then he was of royal blood and would grow to be a brave chief. An ancient prophecy associated with the Naha stone was, he who overturned the rock "shall go forward until all the islands move under his power". (Desha, 2000)

The temple where the Naha stone stood in Hilo was ordered destroyed after Kamehameha's death. The temple's stones were used to build the Haili Church in 1856. The Naha and Pinao stones were too big to use and were covered with foliage before being found and put on display at Hilo Library in 1951. Stephen Desha, a pastor at Hilo's Haili Church, published the story of the Naha stone in his newspaper, Ka Hoku o Hawaii (The Star of Hawaii) in the 1920's. (Thrum, 1907)

Naha and Pinao Stones in front of Hilo Library

Kamehameha's demonstration of strength to turn over the Naha stone gave him fame and support from other chiefs who helped him fulfill the prophecy of ruling all the Hawaii islands.

After passing the Hilo Library on Waianuenue Avenue, turn left on to Kapiolani Street. The Lyman Museum is on the corner of Kapiolani and Haili Street.

7. Lyman Mission House and Museum

Lyman Museum (276 Haili Street) was opened in 1931 to display the Lyman family's collection of rocks, shells, and exhibits on the natural and cultural history of the island. The New England style mission house, next to the museum, is the oldest wooden structure on the island, built in 1839 by David and Sarah Lyman. There is a fee for the museum and guided mission house tour which are open

Monday through Saturday and closed on holidays. (Lyman Museum website)

Lyman Mission House and Museum

David and Sarah Lyman arrived in Hawaii with the fifth company of New England missionaries in 1832. They were assigned to Hilo where they opened a boarding School in 1836. Their students built the wood-framed school and house for the Lymans and their seven children. Sarah Lyman kept records of earthquakes and volcanic eruptions in her journals which are still used by researchers. The school was the first building with electricity in Hilo when a dynamo was installed on the Wailuku River in 1892. (lymanmuseum.com)

St Joseph Catholic Church

Across Kapiolani Street from the Lyman Museum is Saint Joseph Catholic Church built in 1919 for the Portuguese immigrants who moved to Hilo and the growing congregation. (St. Joseph website)

From Lyman Museum, return to Waianuenue Avenue by way of Kapiolani Street and turn left. Drive 1.1 miles, past Hilo High School on the right, to Rainbow Drive and turn right. The parking lot for Rainbow Falls is 0.2 miles on the right.

8. Rainbow Falls and Wailuku River

Rainbow Falls

Rainbow Falls, in Wailuku River State Park, is known for the rainbows in the waterfall mist on sunny days. The overlook is a short walk from the parking area. The amount of water in the waterfall varies from an enormous flow with a thundering roar to a trickle depending on the recent rainfall and snow melt on Mauna Kea. A staircase and path through the trees lead up to an overlook above the falls. Restrooms are located in the parking lot.

According to legend, the cave beneath Rainbow Falls was the home of Hina, a Polynesian goddess. Hina was the mother of Maui, a demi-god best known for conquering the Sun (La) god by tying him down inside his house (the Hale a ke La) on the island of Maui, until he agreed to go slower each day for half the year to allow his mother, Hina, enough time to dry her kapa cloth in a single day. (Reed, 1987)

Moo Kuna, a giant lizard, often harassed Hina by throwing logs and rocks into the river. One day Kuna blocked the river with a huge rock to flood Hina's cave. Hina cried to Maui, who was fishing in his canoe and in two strokes he crashed his canoe at the mouth of the Wailuku River (see Maui's Canoe in the Downtown Hilo Walking Tour). With his magic club he had used to conquer the sun god La, Maui struck the huge rock and cracked it in two. The remains of the huge boulder, called Lonokaeho, are covered with plants where water still rushes past it. Kuna fled to a hiding place up the river, but Maui came after him. They waged battle up and down the Wailuku River with Kuna sliding away each time by diving from one pool to another. Maui called upon Pele, the goddess of the volcano for help. Pele pelted hot stones and lava onto the pools until the water boiled and the scalding water killed Kuna. Maui rolled Kuna's dead body to a spot below his mother's cave in Rainbow Falls, where the black rock island, called Moo Kuna, still is today. (James 1995)

Another entrance to the 16 acre Wailuku River Park is located about 1.4 miles further up Waianuenue Avenue from the Rainbow Falls parking area. The second entrance is next to Boiling Pots and Peepee Falls with an overlook near the parking area. The lava outcrops in the river channel directly below the overlook are from a Mauna Loa lava flow about 3500 years ago. Lava pillows on the opposite bank were formed when the lava entered deep water. (Hazlett, 1996)

The footpath below the overlook to the Boiling Pots is slippery and dangerous to walk down and it is not advisable to swim in the Wailuku River.

The Wailuku River drains from pool to pool through underground lava tubes and cracks. If the water level is low, the water may disappear entirely into the plunge pools. When enough water is flowing in the river, the water swirls and spins around inside the tubes and resembles boiling water.

HILO DOWNTOWN WALKING TOUR

Hilo Downtown Boardwalk

Downtown Hilo has shops, museums, bookstores, and restaurants along covered walkways from the Farmer's Market on Mamo Street to Waianuenue Avenue. The maze of one-way streets in downtown makes it difficult to drive around the area. The short distances on flat sidewalks in downtown Hilo makes it relatively easy to walk with many places to stop and rest.

In early times, the downtown area had settlements and temples along the Wailuku River. The sugar boom in the early 1900's brought businesses and commerce to Hilo. Tsunamis in 1946 and 1960 destroyed portions of the downtown but many of the buildings constructed during the boom survived and have been refurbished for new businesses. This walking tour has 11 stops over approximately

0.5 miles and 0.3 miles to return to the starting point at Mooheau Park.

1. Mooheau Park
2. Farmer's Market
3. S. Hata Building
4. S.H. Kress Building
5. Pacific Tsunami Museum
6. East Hawaii Cultural Center
7. Kalakaua Park
8. Federal Building
9. Puueo Bridge & Maui's Canoe
10. Hilo Armory
11. Koehnen Bldg/Mokupapapa Center

Hilo Downtown Map and Walking Tour

1. Mooheau Park

Mooheau Park and Bus Station

Mooheau Park (231 Kamehameha Avenue) is located between Hilo Bayfront and downtown. It has the largest parking lot near downtown and is across the street from the Farmer's Market. Mooheau Park was opened in 1905 with a pavilion donated by George Beckley. The Hilo Band celebrated the grand opening with music composed by Hilo's Joaquin Carvalho called the "Mooheau March". (Langton, 1905) The bandstand is used for performances and events. The park has a terminal for the island's public bus, Hele-On, and a visitor information center.

2. Hilo Farmer's Market

Hilo Farmer's Market

Farmer's Market (400 Kamehameha Avenue) is on the corner of Mamo Street across from Mooheau Park. The open-air market has dozens of vendors selling produce every day and on Wednesdays and Saturdays the market grows in size with over 200 farmers and local craft vendors. A colorful array of tropical fruits, nuts, and vegetables are on display under a tarp covering. Orchids, anthuriums, coffee, jams, honey, bakery items, and local foods are also for sale. (Hilo Farmer's Market website)

3. S. Hata Building

From the Farmer's Market walk under the covered walkway to the historic two-story S. Hata building (308 Kamehameha Avenue). The concrete building was constructed in 1912 and restored in the 1990's for restaurants, stores, and art galleries.

Covered walkway in front of Hata Building

Sadanosuke Hata built his new store on Front Street, later renamed Kamehameha Avenue, near the railroad tracks on Hilo's bayfront. Hata bought the property under the condition that the building be made of concrete, rather than wood like most of the other buildings in Hilo. In 1913, he opened Hilo Sake Brewing Company upstairs above his store. The reinforced concrete building survived two major tsunamis. (Hunter,hawaiitribune-hearld.com/sections/news/local-news/s-hata-building-marks-100-years.html)

Hata's brother Yoichi Hata started Y Hata & Co. in 1913, a family-owned food service distribution company in Hawaii. (yhata.com)

Continue under the covered walkway, past the natural food store and cross Furneaux Street. The covered walkway continues next to the Old American Bakery Building and Hilo Bay Building. At the end of the block, cross Haili Street and find the Kress Building in the middle of the block before Kalakaua Street.

4. S.H. Kress Building

The three story S. H. Kress (174 Kamehameha Avenue) was built in 1932 and renovated in 1995 for use as a cinema, operated by Hollywood Theaters, and a charter school.

The building was designed for a national chain of Kress five and dime retail stores in an art deco style using a brown terra cotta façade. Samuel Kress viewed his stores as "public art" and hired architects to design his 250 stores which have become landmarks in the business districts of towns in 29 states. The store and fountain operated for almost 50 years in Hilo before closing in 1980. (Kress foundation website)

S.H Kress Building

5. Pacific Tsunami Museum

    The Pacific Tsunami Museum (130 Kamehameha Avenue) is across Kalakaua Street from the Kress building. The museum was opened to archive the history and oral stories of residents who survived the tsunamis that devastated Hilo and to educate current residents about how to stay safe during future tsunamis. Displays and videos in the museum show the downtown and residential areas of Hilo before and after the major 1946 and 1960 tsunamis. The museum also has exhibits about the science of tsunamis and how they are formed.

    There is an entrance fee for the museum which is open Monday through Saturday. Their website maintains information and resources and has an online tour of tsunami memorial sites around Hilo. (Tsunami Museum website)

Pacific Tsunami Museum facing Hilo Bay

The Tsunami Museum building was originally the First Hawaiian Bank built in 1930 and designed by CW Dickey with a Renaissance revival architecture. The bank donated the building to the museum in 1997. The museum's movie theater was the bank vault. (tsunami.org/historical.html)

On the same block as the Tsunami Museum, between Kalakaua Street and Waianuenue Avenue, is the Sig Zane clothing store (122 Kamehameha Avenue) with his famous designs inspired by Hawaiian flowers and ferns. (Sig Zane website)

Looking toward Hilo Bay from the sidewalk in front of Sig Zane's store, a white lighthouse and stand of coconut trees are visible on a small peninsula in Hilo Bay at the end of Waianuenue Avenue. This location is called Kaipalaoa Landing which is said to have been King Kamehameha's favorite surfing spot. In 1863 and 1890, wharves were built on the peninsula for passengers and freight to be loaded onto steamers anchored in Hilo Bay. Bayfront road (Highway 19) sits on railroad land where trains to Hilo once operated from 1899 to 1946.

Kaipalaoa Landing at the end of Waianuenue Avenue

From the Tsunami Museum, walk inland from Hilo Bay along Kalakaua Street for two blocks to the East Hawaii Cultural Center.

6. East Hawaii Cultural Center

East Hawaii Cultural Center and Dickey building

The East Hawaii Cultural Center (141 Kalakaua Street) has art exhibits, classes, workshops, and shows in its galleries and small theaters. The center is open Monday through Saturday and special events are listed on their website. (EHCC website)

The East Hawaii Cultural Center was Hilo's District Courthouse and Police Station until 1975. It was designed by Frank Arakawa and constructed in 1932 with reinforced concrete, a wooden interior, and a hip roof to look like an early Hawaiian house.

An empty, two story, brown cinder block building next to the Cultural Center was built by CW Dickey in 1929 for the Hawaiian Telephone Company. This building is an example of Hawaiian Regional Architecture with a green tiled roof and colorful terracotta tiles set into the building. (downtownhilo.com)

7. Kalakaua Park

Banyan Tree in Kalakaua Park

Kalakaua Park is across from the East Hawaii Cultural Center with the Federal Building on the opposite side. This area was once the town center of Hilo with important buildings surrounding it. A huge banyan tree is next to the statue of King David Kalakaua which holds an ipu (a gourd drum used for hula and chants) and a taro leaf (the plant used to make poi). King Kalakaua was known as the Merrie Monarch because of the many gala events he held during his reign from 1874 to 1891.The bronze sundial in the park was donated to Hilo by King Kalakaua in 1877 and has the royal coat of arms.

In 1991, a time capsule was buried in the park during a total solar eclipse to be opened during the next solar eclipse in Hilo. Along the side of Kalakaua Park is a war memorial with a walkway along a huge koi pond between Kalakaua Street and Waianuenue Avenue.

Statue of King David Kalakaua in Kalakaua Park

    The property next to Kalakaua Park, across Kinoole Street where the dilapidated Hilo Hotel now sits, was called Niolopa and used as a retreat by the royal families of Hawaii. Liholiho, King Kamehameha's eldest son, stayed at Niolopa when it was a large grass house. Liholiho was born in Hilo in 1797 and succeeded his father as King Kamehameha II in 1819.

    In 1824, the thatched Waiakea Mission church (the first church in Hilo) was moved from its first location to the site of Kalakaua Park. (hailichurch.org)

    In 1840, Benjamin Pitman, a businessman from Boston, built a house on the Niolopa property for his wife, Kinooleoliliha, the daughter of high chief, Hoolulu. Kinoole inherited most of the land in Hilo. The

Pitmans moved to Honolulu, where Kinoole died in 1855, at the age of twenty-eight. (Merry, 2000)

Queen Liliuokalani, the last monarch of Hawaii also stayed at Niolopa. The Queen and Mrs. Rufus Lyman were family and when Liliuokalani came to Hilo, she and her retainers would walk on a grassy path from Niolopa to the Lyman house which came to be known as the Queen's Walk. (hilounionschool.org/ourpages)

In Godfrey's 1899 Guide to Hilo, he describes Hilo as the "Queen City of Hawaii". The Hilo Hotel on Pitman Street (now Kinoole Street) had rooms with views of Hilo Bay. The sundial, given by King Kalakaua, was placed near a large flagstaff in the center of the grounds, now Kalakaua Park.(Godfrey, 1899). Lycurgus (who owned Volcano House at the time) bought Hilo Hotel in 1908 from John D. Spreckels.

8. Federal Building

Hilo Federal Building and Post Office

The Federal Building (154 Waianuenue Avenue) is across from Kalakaua Park. US Postal service was started in Hilo in 1858, but the federal building was not finished until 1917. The New York architect Henry Whitfield designed the building in the Mediterranean Renaissance Revival style, to blend traditional classical architecture with features suited to a tropical climate. The reinforced concrete building with a green tile roof originally functioned as a courthouse, post office, and custom house. It also housed immigration, agriculture service, the weather bureau and the IRS. Two wings were added between 1936 and 1938. A two story colonnade is supported by tall Tuscan columns and colorful mosaic tiles and urns add to the style.

From Waianuenue Avenue, walk along the side of the Federal Building on Kekaulike Street where the American Legion planted 17 royal palms in 1922 to honor Hawaiian citizens who died in World War I. Name markers are located under the trees. (gsa.gov/portal/ext/html/site/hb/category/25431/actionParameter/exploreByBuilding/buildingId/550)

Turn right where Kekaulike Street ends at the Wailuku River, on to Wailuku Drive. The Puueo Bridge is one block from Kekaulike Street along the river at Keawe Street.

9. Puueo Bridge and Maui's Canoe

Puueo Street Bridge

The Puueo Street bridge is one of three bridges that cross the Wailuku River in Hilo. Wailuku means "destructive water" and the river has caused floods, property destruction, and deaths in the past. In 1901, a hydro electric power station was built on the Wailuku to generate electricity for Hilo and to make ice.

From the middle of the bridge, looking toward Hilo Bay, you can see the Highway 19 bridge called the "Singing Bridge" for the humming sound made by tires on the metal grid. A railroad bridge crossed the Wailuku River where the Singing Bridge now stands, but it was destroyed by the 1946 tsunami.

Maui's Canoe in the Wailuku River

Looking the opposite direction from Hilo Bay, towards the Wainaku Street Bridge, "Maui's Canoe" can be seen in the river. Ka Waa O Maui (the canoe of Maui) is a long black lava island shaped like a canoe located in the Wailuku River on the left side. It is said that the lava island is the remains of the demigod Maui's canoe when he rushed to rescue his mother, the goddess Hina. (James, 1995) See Rainbow Falls in the Hilo Driving Tour section for more about Hina and her battle with a giant lizard creature on the Wailuku River.

From the Puueo Bridge, walk back to Wailuku Drive. The imposing Hilo Armory building is between Wailuku Drive and Shipman Street in the direction of Hilo Bay.

10. Hilo Armory and Kaipalaoa Heiau

The Hilo Armory (28 Shipman Street) is located in an area known as Piihonua. In 1917, the Territory of Hawaii built the Armory to store military supplies and equipment issued by the US government. (Forbes, 1917) Now the building is used by the Hawaii County Parks and Recreation department for youth sports, physical fitness classes, and arts and crafts. The original Merrie Monarch festival in 1964 took place in the Hilo Armory along with the coronation pageant.

The land where the Armory sits was once the site of an important temple called Kaipalaoa Heiau. The Naha Stone and Pinao Stone, located in front of the Hilo Public Library (see Naha Stone on Hilo Driving Tour) were part of this temple. When Kamehameha was young he visited Kaipalaoa Heiau to fulfill the prophecy that the one who upends the Naha stone will rule all of Hawaii. In 1797, Kamehameha's eldest son, Liholiho (who became King Kamehameha II) had his navel cord cutting ceremony at this location. The temple was destroyed after King Kamehameha died in 1819 and his wife Queen Kaahumanu and son Liholiho issued an edict to burn the idols and destroy the temples of the old Hawaiian religion. In 1856, the stones from the rubble of the temple were used to build the Haili Church on 211 Haili Street. (Thrum, 1906)

Hilo Armory Building

The most important occurrence at Kaipalaoa Heiau was the proclamation by King Kamehameha of the "Law of the Splintered Paddle" (Ke Kanawai Mamalahoe). The law was prompted by an incident in Puna where Kamehameha planned a raid of his enemies from his base in Laupahoehoe. The fisherman saw the warriors arrive and ran as Kamehameha jumped from his canoe to pursue them. Kamehameha's foot became trapped in a lava crevice and he was stuck and completely exposed. The fisherman returned and began to attack him. A fisherman whacked Kamehameha with a paddle that splintered into pieces and knocked him out. His warriors were able to fend off the attackers, free his foot from the crevice, and retreat. When Kamehameha later became King of Hawaii Island, the chiefs brought the Puna fisherman before him for punishment. King Kamehameha forgave the fisherman and made what many consider the most important royal edict of his reign, known as the Law of the Splintered Paddle:

"Oh my people, honor thy gods, respect alike men great and humble; see to it that our aged, our women, and our children lie down to sleep by the roadside without fear of harm. Disobey and die."

This law was included in Hawaii's 1978 State Constitution. (Clark, 1985)

The Koehnen Building is on Hilo Bayfront in front of the Armory.

11. Koehnen Bldg/Mokupapapa Discovery Center

Koehnen Building

The Mokupapapa Discovery Center recently moved to the Koehnen Building (76 Kamehameha Ave). The Center was created to educate people about the remote coral reefs in the Papahanaumokuakea Marine National Monument northwest of the Hawaiian Islands. It is the largest conservation area in the US covering 139,797 square miles of the Pacific Ocean. The center has maps, exhibits and a large saltwater aquarium. (Mokupapapa Discovery Center website)

    The Kohenen Building was built by H. Hackfield in 1910 in a Renaissance Revival style. The building was used by American Factors and sold to the Kohenen family in 1957 for their furniture store which closed in 2013.
(sanctuaries.noaa.gov/news/press/2013/pr040313.html)

HILO AREA BEACHES AND GARDENS

Highway 19 north of Hilo

Tropical gardens, plantations, waterfalls, and rugged, black lava beaches are just a short drive from Hilo. This section has directions and descriptions of unique places near Hilo to experience more of what the Hilo area has to offer.

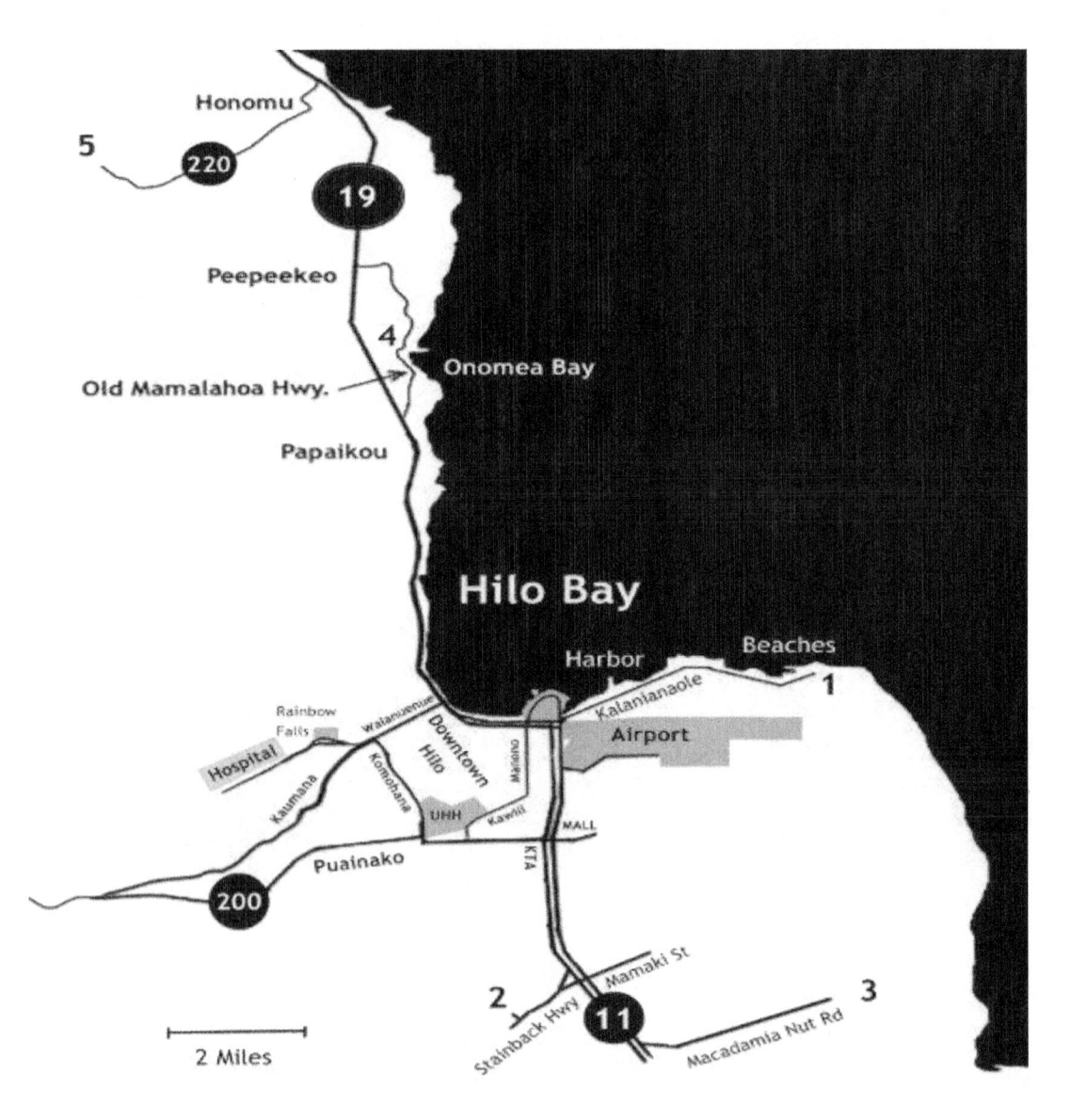

1. Richardson Ocean Center
2. Panaewa Rainforest Zoo
3. Mauna Loa Macadamia Nut Farm
4. Hawaii Tropical Botanical Garden
5. Akaka Falls State Park

Hilo Area Beaches and Gardens Map

1. Richardson Ocean Center and Hilo Beaches

Leleiwi Beach Park and Richardson Ocean Center

Hilo's beach parks are located along Kalanianaole Avenue south of Hilo Bay. The beaches are exposed to the open ocean and offer great views of the crashing waves on the black lava coastline. Kalanianaole Avenue starts at the intersection of Highway 11 and Highway 19 and ends at Leleiwi Beach Park.

The first beach, south of Hilo Harbor and the Aloha petroleum storage tanks, is Keaukaha Beach Park. The park is 1.3 miles from the start of Kalanianaole Avenue and mostly undeveloped and used by residents for fishing. The next beach park is Onekahakaha, which means "drawing in the sand". The park was dedicated in the 1930's and is one of the few beaches with white sand. The area has dangerous currents but there is a sandy pool protected by a boulder that residents use. James Kealoha Beach Park, dedicated in 1963 in honor of the first Lt. Governor of the State of Hawaii, is located a half mile further south. This park has a few small protected swimming areas which are somewhat safe from the hazardous currents. The water is extremely cold from fresh water springs.

At the end of Kalanianaole Avenue is Leleiwi Beach Park, a large ocean area that includes Richardson Ocean Center. This beach is considered the best snorkeling beach in Hilo. There is a protected inlet in the center of the park, but the safest snorkeling is in the sheltered bay bordering Richardson Ocean Center near the lifeguard stands. The bay has a variety of fish and marine life.

The Richardson Ocean Center houses the county aquatics operation which manages the island's public swimming pools and lifeguards. The facilities include picnic pavilions, showers, restrooms, paved walkways, and several parking lots.

Richardson Ocean Center

The Ocean Center was the residence of George and Elsa Richardson who lived on the Malo family's property. The first Malo, Kauikoaole, moved to the Leleiwi property in the late 1800's. Kauikoaole's son, David, shortened his name to Malo after he had a dream about it. In 1920, the entire family came down with typhoid fever. Malo's wife was able to walk to the home of George Richardson on Reed's Bay to get help. In gratitude for his help, Malo invited Richardson to live on his property. Malo designed Richardson's house with large doors on both sides to allow water to rush through during storms and tsunamis which saved the house many times. (Clark, 1985)

2. Panaewa Rainforest Zoo

Hilo's zoo has a small collection of animals within a well maintained garden in a rainforest area on the border of Hilo and Puna. Paved paths are lined with colorful bamboo, palm trees, and orchids. There are more than 80 species of birds, animals, reptiles, and insects, many of them from the tropics.

Paved pathways in the Hilo Zoo

The zoo is free and is open daily, except Christmas and New Years Day. At the entrance is a lily pond and gift store with stroller rentals. The zoo has a playground, picnic tables, and a petting zoo open on Saturday afternoons. It is easy to spend an hour or half a day strolling through the gardens and viewing the zoo exhibits. (Hilo Zoo website)

Birds cages at the Hilo Zoo

The zoo is located on Stainback Highway past the Equestrian Center Complex. From Hilo's Prince Kuhio Plaza, drive 2.5 miles on Highway 11 toward Volcano and turn right on to Mamaki Street. If you are coming from Volcano toward Hilo, turn left across Highway 11 at Mamaki. Mamaki Street ends at Stainback Highway. Turn left on to Stainback and the zoo entrance is approximately one half mile down the road.

Panaewa is a Hawaiian name that refers to the tropical rainforest which borders the Hilo and Puna districts. Panaewa is mentioned in Hawaiian legends as the forest and the treacherous moo (lizard) god Panaewa who lived there and ate travelers on the path between Hilo and Puna. Hiiaka, the sister of the volcano goddess Pele, challenged

Panaewa and was victorious and made the trail through the Panaewa forest safe.

The Panaewa forest is mentioned in Hawaiian chants and songs with descriptions of its huge ohia and lehua trees and special plants that are used to make traditional leis. Maile vines with shiny fragrant leaves are found in the forest and used to make leis given to signify respect and honor. The silvery green leaves of the painiu plant found in the forest are also used in lei making. (hawaii.edu/hawaiian/KHaili/Panaewa.htm)

3. Mauna Loa Macadamia Nut Farm

The Mauna Loa Macadamia Nut Farm is located south of Hilo on Macadamia Nut Road. The visitor center has samples of nuts and candies, a store, snack bar, restrooms, and a garden. The factory, where the nuts are processed and the chocolates are made, has a self-guided tour from an outside walkway accessible by stairs.

Mauna Loa Macadamia Nut Factory

The visitor center is free and open Monday through Saturday, closed on holidays. From Hilo's Prince Kuhio Plaza, drive 4 miles on Highway 11 toward Volcano and turn left across the highway onto Macadamia Nut Road. If you are coming from Volcano toward Hilo, turn right on Macadamia Nut Road. The visitor center and factory are 3 miles down Macadamia Nut Road through acres of macadamia nut trees. (Mauna Loa Nut website)

4. Hawaii Tropical Botanical Garden

Onomea Falls in Hawaii Tropical Botanical Garden

Hawaii Tropical Botanical Garden is operated by a non-profit organization preserving thousands of tropical plant species on their 40 acres above beautiful Onomea Bay. Since the property is a cliff above the ocean, a 500 foot long boardwalk was built to get down the steep cliff to the gardens below.

500 foot boardwalk down to the tropical gardens

At the bottom of the boardwalk are trails through the garden's palm trees, colorful heliconias, orchids, bromeliads, anthuriums, and water lilies. At the end of the path is a dramatic view of Onomea Bay. Photographers and flower lovers will find the tropical garden a spectacular place to spend a half day or more.

The garden has an admission charge and is open daily except holidays. The self guided tour from the visitors center and back is about a mile. A ride up the boardwalk on a golf cart is available for a fee.

From Hilo, drive 7 miles north on Highway 19 to Papaikou. Turn toward the ocean between mile marker 7 and 8 on to Old Mamalahoa Highway. The visitor center is about 1.5 miles down the road. (Hawaii Tropical Botanical Garden website)

5. Akaka Falls State Park

Akaka Waterfall

Akaka Falls State Park has two fantastic waterfalls and a nature walk through a tropical forest. Akaka Falls is the most dramatic waterfall with a 442 foot drop into a pool of water. The smaller 100 foot Kahuna Falls can be seen on a 0.5 mile paved trail through dense tropical vegetation. The state park is open daily and charges a parking fee for non-residents.

A short paved path with a sign labeled "Akaka Falls Only" goes directly to the overlook of Akaka Falls. The path has stairs and is not wheelchair accessible, but is fairly easy to walk. The longer nature walk takes about 30 minutes and leads past bamboo, ferns, vines, orchids, and across bridges over miniature waterfalls.

Seventy feet above the bottom of Akaka Falls is a stone called Kaloa, named for the 3 nights of the month sacred to the god Kanaloa. Another stone called Pohaku o Pele is located in the stream under the falls and is said to make the sky dark and the rain fall if struck with a branch. (James, 1995)

Akaka Falls is located on Highway 220 off Highway 19 between mile markers 13 and 14. From Hilo, turn left on Highway 220 and drive through the town of Honomu. Highway 220 ends at the parking lot for Akaka Falls State Park. (Hawaii Island State Parks website)

Akaka Falls State Park Nature Walk

Events and Festivals in Hilo

Annual Festivals in Hilo

Ellison Onizuka Science Day (January)
Chinese New Year Festival (February)
International Nights University of Hawaii Hilo (February)
Big Island International Marathon (March)
Merrie Monarch Hula Festival (April)
Lei Day (May)
Inter-Tribal Pow Wow (May)
Taiko Drum Festival (June)
Kamehameha Day Festival (June)
Hilo Bay Blast (4th July)
Big Island Music Festival (July)
OBon Dances at Buddhist Temples (July-August)
Hilo Orchid Society (August)
Liliuokalani Festival (September)
Hilo Downtown Hoolaulea Music Festival (September)
Wayfinding Festival (September)
Big Island Ukulele Guild Exhibition (October)
Taste of Hilo (October)
Black and White Night Downtown Hilo (November)
Veterans Day Parade (November)
Mystery of the Christmas Star (December)

Imiloa Astronomy Center and Planetarium

Regular Events and Activities in Hilo

Imiloa Astronomy Center planetarium
Roller Derby
University of Hawaii Performing Arts Center
East Hawaii Cultural Center
Naniloa Volcanoes Golf Club (120 Banyan Drive).
Prince Kuhio Plaza indoor mall
University of Hilo Vulcan games
Kawamoto Swim Stadium (260 Kalanikoa Street)
BJ Penn Training and Fitness (639 Kinoole Street)
Stars Pro Baseball
Hilo Motor Speedway Races

CHAPTER 4: VOLCANOES NATIONAL PARK

Kilauea Volcano

Hawaii Volcanoes National Park is over 333,000 acres stretching from the coastline to the summits of Mauna Loa and Kilauea Volcanoes. Kilauea Volcano has been continuously erupting since 1983 with lava flows that start and stop and move from within the park to private lands in Puna. The entrance to Volcanoes National Park is on Highway 11 between mile markers 28 and 29. It is open 24 hours a day every day of the year. The park charges a fee to enter. (Volcanoes National Park website)

Volcanoes National Park has scenic views and hiking trails at an elevation of 4,000 feet where it is often cool and rainy. The nearby residential areas of Volcano have places to stay, restaurants, a winery, and a golf course.

Entrance to Hawaii Volcanoes National Park on Highway 11

If you have only a few hours to spend in the park on a drive around the island, the best places to get an overview of the park is at the Visitor Center, Volcano House lookout, and the Jaggar Museum.

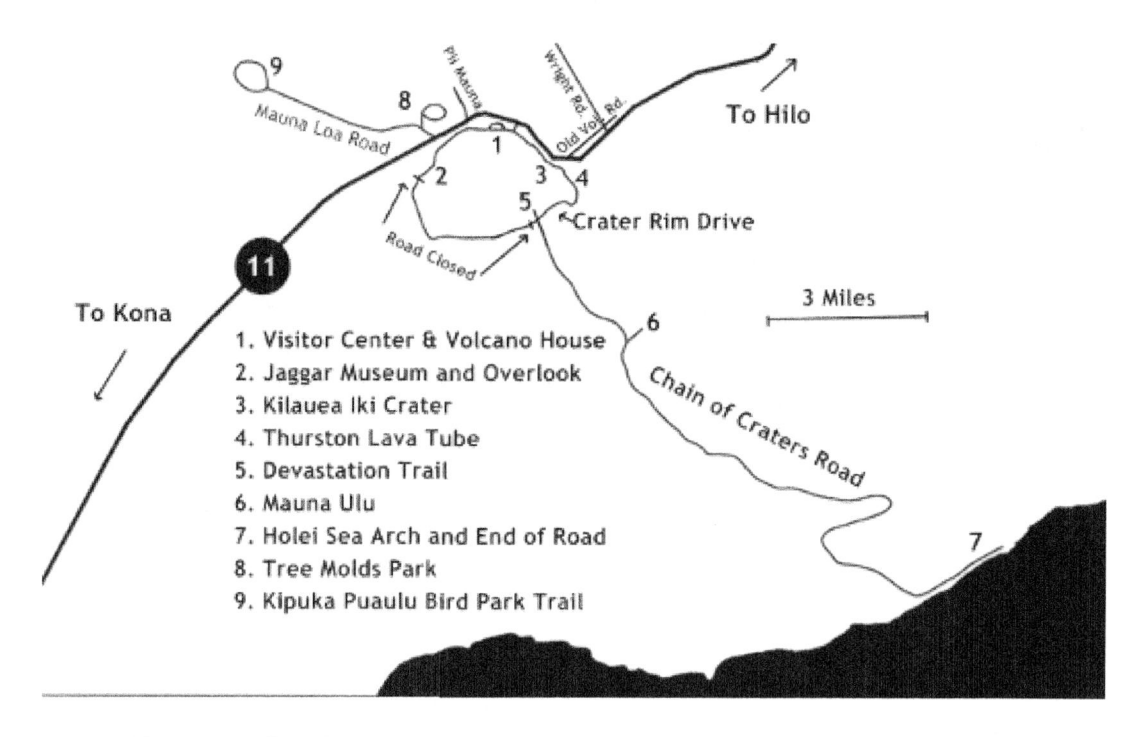

Hawaii Volcanoes National Park Map and Sites

1. Visitor Center & Volcano House
2. Jaggar Museum and Overlook
3. Kilauea Iki Crater
4. Thurston Lava Tube
5. Devastation Trail
6. Mauna Ulu
7. Holei Sea Arch and End of Road
8. Tree Molds Park
9. Kipuka Puaulu Bird Park Trail

1. Kilauea Visitor Center and Volcano House

The Kilauea Visitor Center is 0.2 miles from the park entrance on the right side of Crater Rim Road. The center has informative exhibits, a book store, and movies showing in a theater. An activities bulletin board with information about ranger led programs is near the entrance and volunteers are available to answer questions about the volcano and sites in the park. (Volcanoes National Park website)

Kilauea Visitor Center

    Volcano Art Center is next to the Kilauea Visitor Center in a building that was the Volcano House Hotel in 1877 with the original fireplace. The gallery has art work by local artisans. (Volcano Art Center website) The first Volcano House was made from grass in 1846. It was rebuilt in 1866, the year Mark Twain was a guest.

Volcano Art Center in the old Volcano House

Across the road from the Visitor Center is Volcano House which is located on the rim of the volcano's caldera with an excellent viewpoint. The lobby has plate glass windows where spewing gases from Halemaumau Crater can be seen. There is also a viewing area outside. Volcano house has restaurants, gift stores, and guest rooms with views of the volcano. (Volcano House website)

Volcano House across from the Visitor Center

George and Demosthenes Lycurgus took over management of Volcano House in 1904. George was tricked into coming to Hawaii in 1889 by the Spreckels brothers who owned the Oceanic Steam Company and wanted help with their banana business. They entertained him onboard in San Francisco and left the port for Hawaii without him noticing. After only a brief time in Hawaii he returned a year later. George opened a hotel in Honolulu and entertained Robert Louis Stevenson, Jack London, and other renowned guests. After a visit to Kilauea, he became interested in Volcano House and sent for his nephew Demosthenes in Greece, who managed Volcano House from 1904 to 1919. George repurchased the Volcano House property in 1932, 11 years after selling it. The volcano had been quiet for years and the hotel was empty. The story goes that on September 5, 1934, George and his friend Lancaster, a Cherokee Indian, walked down to Halemaumau Crater, said some prayers to the volcano goddess Pele and threw in a lei and a bottle of gin, partially drained. A few hours after they went to bed, the volcano erupted for the first time in four years. The 1934 eruption lasted for only a month but the visitors to Volcano House helped keep the operation going. When the 1952 eruption started, 93 year old George Lycurgus rode to the edge of the crater on horseback and threw in his offering of a lei and bottle of gin. (nps.gov/history/history/online_books/hawaii-notes/vol5-2d.htm)

2. Jaggar Museum and Halemaumau Lookout

Jaggar Museum lookout over Halemaumau Crater

    Jaggar museum has exhibits about volcanoes and a gift shop. The museum's lookout has the closest view of Halemaumau Crater. (Jaggar Museum website)

    From the Visitor Center, turn right onto Crater Rim Drive to drive to Jaggar Museum. The road passes through a treeless area where steam can be seen rising from the ground. The steam vent parking lot is located 0.8 miles from the Visitor Center next to Steaming Bluff trail which leads to the edge of the caldera. Vents surrounded by metal rails in the parking lot, release clouds of steam into the cool air. Kilauea Military Camp, a hotel for military personnel, is on the right 1.1 miles from the Visitor Center. Jaggar Museum's parking lot is located 2.6 miles from the Visitor Center on Crater Rim Drive. Restrooms are located near the parking lot.

The museum is located next to the USGS Hawaiian Volcano Observatory (HVO) which was started by Dr. Thomas Jaggar in 1912. HVO monitors the activity of the volcanoes and lava flows on the island. (HVO website)

The portion of Crater Rim Drive beyond Jaggar Museum is closed. From the Jaggar Museum parking lot, turn right to return to the Visitor Center. Continue on the road and turn right before the park entrance to view other sites on Crater Rim Drive.

3. Kilauea Iki Crater

View into the crater from Kilauea Iki parking lot

Kilauea Iki Crater is within the Kilauea Caldera and was active in 1959. The bottom of the crater is 380 feet below and can be seen from the fence at the edge of the parking lot. Hikers on a trail at the bottom of the crater look tiny from the view above.

The Kilauea Iki Crater parking lot is located 1.4 miles from the Visitor Center past the park entrance through a thick fern forest on Crater Rim Drive. A flat, half mile trail through lush vegetation starts at the Kilauea Iki parking lot and goes to the Thurston Lava Tube parking lot.

4. Thurston Lava Tube

Thurston Lava Tube is a cave created from a lava flow with a picturesque walkway through it. The loop trail is one third of a mile and leads down steps to a dense fern forest and through the lighted lava tunnel

The Thurston Lava Tube parking lot is a 0.4 mile drive from the Kilauea Iki Crater parking lot on Crater Rim Drive. The parking lot is often crowded with tour busses and visitors to the popular landmark.

Walkway into Thurston Lava Tube

The lava tube was discovered by Lorrin A. Thurston, grandson of the missionaries Asa and Lucy Thurston who arrived in Kona with the first group of missionaries in 1820. Lorrin Thurston was a lawyer and publisher of the Honolulu Advertiser newspaper. He and his associates

bought Volcano House in 1891 and remodeled and expanded the old hotel. In 1913, during one of his stays at the volcano, he discovered the lava cave, called Nahuku, with his niece and Dr. Jaggar.

Thurston worked for a decade to get Kilauea, Mauna Loa, and Haleakala Volcanoes into the national park system. He was supported by Dr. Jaggar and Prince Jonah Kuhio, who was the Territory of Hawaii's representative to Congress. A group of Congressmen visited the volcano in 1915 and Thurston accompanied them to make a case for a national park and get federal funding for the Jaggar's Volcano Observatory. Finally, the money was found to buy the private land and President Wilson signed a law making Hawaii Volcanoes the 11th National Park in 1916. (nps.gov/history/history/online_books/hawaii-notes/vol5-2h.htm)

5. Devastation Trail

Devastation Trail goes across a field of cinder created from the 1959 eruption of Kilauea Iki. The paved trail is one half mile from the Devastation Trail parking lot to the Puu Puai Overlook. To see the cinder field, it is just a short walk on the trail from the parking lot through a forest area.

The Devastation Trail parking lot is located at the end of Crater Rim Drive 1.4 miles from the Thurston Lava Tube parking lot.

Devastation Trail

The **Chain of Craters Road** is 20 miles in length and descends 3700 feet to the coast where it dead ends at a 2003 lava flow that covered the road. The start of the Chain of Craters Road is across from the Devastation Trail parking lot. It takes at least an hour to drive to the end of the road and back. There are no gasoline stations and limited cell phone service on the road. A vendor with food and drinks is sometimes open at the end of the road.

Starting at the top of the Chain of Craters Road, the road passes by turnouts at the Lua Manu Crater, Puhimau Crater, Kookoolau Crater, and Pauahi Crater.

6. Mauna Ulu

Mauna Ulu is a large shield vent which erupted starting in 1969 and created a desolate lava field all the way to the ocean. The turn off to the Mauna Ulu parking area is 4.2 miles from the top of the Chain of Craters Road. The 0.6 mile section of road leading to the parking area was the original Chain of Craters Road covered by Mauna Ulu lava flows.

Lava flow covered the road at Mauna Ulu

From the parking lot it is a short walk to a sign that marks the front of the 1974 lava flow. The Mauna Ulu Eruption Trail is a tenth of a mile and starts in the parking lot. The trail goes through a forest to the 1969 eruption fissure. The rock formations are unusual with some bright colored lava rocks and fissures with ferns growing in the sterile cinder landscape.

Continuing on the drive, there is a viewing platform that overlooks the lava field and Puna coastline located 8.3 miles from the start of the Chain of Craters Road.

Viewing platform over the ocean at Muliwai a Pele

A second viewing platform and picnic area on a cliff overlooking the ocean at Kealakomo, is 10.7 miles from the start of the Chain of Craters Road. The road then zigzags down the steep cliff called Holei Pali.

Pahoehoe Lava swirl

Though pahoehoe lava has a smooth, ropy surface and aa lava is jagged with a clinkery surface, they are made of the same type of rocks.

Pahoehoe is created by lava that is hotter and its smooth surface with wrinkles and folds is easy to walk on. Aa lava is created when cooler lava breaks into sharp rubble. Its surface is difficult to walk on and cuts up shoes.

The parking area for Puu Loa petroglyph trail is 17 miles from the top of the Chain of Craters Road. The one mile trail leads to a creaky, wooden platform that overlooks petroglyphs in the lava. The trail is on sharp, rugged lava with no shade.

7. Holei Sea Arch and End of the Road

60 foot tall Holei Sea Arch

The Holei Sea Arch is at the end of the Chain of Craters Road. There is no parking lot; vehicles park along the side of the road where the road is barricaded. The arch can be seen by walking toward the ocean down to a viewing platform. Picnic tables, portable toilets, and a food vendor are located on the road.

End of Chain of Craters Road covered with lava

The 2003 lava flow across the Chain of Craters Road is a half mile down the road from where the road is barricaded. It is a mile walk on flat pavement round trip to see the old lava flow that destroyed the road that used to go to Volcanoes National Park's second entrance in Kalapana, Puna.

8. Volcano Tree Molds park

Tree Molds created by lava flows

Volcano Lava Tree Molds is in Hawaii Volcanoes National Park but located outside of the park entrance on Mauna Loa Road. From Highway 11 and the park entrance, drive 2.3 miles toward Kona and turn right on to Mauna Loa Road. Turn right on to Tree Molds Road. The narrow road twists and turns for about a half mile to a one-way loop road. Near the end of the loop is a small parking area. A short trail goes through a group of lava tree molds. Most of the deep holes have railings around them, but not all of them and some holes are hidden off the trail. The park has no facilities.

Lava trees and lava molds are both formed by molten lava hitting trees and hardening around them as it cools. The hot lava burns the tree and leaves a hollow inside the lava. If the lava drains out of the forest area, a lava tree is left behind. If the lava does not drain out, a mold or hole is left where the tree once stood. Tree molds are less common than lava trees because of the exact conditions required and the likelihood that a later lava flow will fill the holes. (Thrum, 1907)

9. Kipuka Puaulu Bird Park Trail

Start of Kipuka Puaulu Bird Park trail

Kipuka Puaulu is an old-growth forest surrounded by lava flows. The Kipuka Puaulu Bird Park is located on Mauna Loa Road past Tree Molds Road, 1.5 miles from Highway 11. The park has a one mile loop trail through a forest of ferns, ohia, koa, and other native trees. Koa trees along the path have bright orange algae growing on their trunks. A 73 foot tall Manele tree (soapberry) in the park is the tallest recorded in the US.

After parking on the circular drive, walk past the wooden sign along the path to the loop trail. Restrooms and picnic tables are located near the trailhead. A narrow road from the Bird Park circle drive goes 10 miles up the slope of Mauna Loa to a scenic lookout.

Between Mauna Loa Road and the Hawaii Volcanoes National Park entrance is Pii Mauna Drive where the Volcano Golf and

Country Club and Volcano Winery are located. (Volcano Winery website and Volcano Golf and Country Club website)

Volcano Village is on Old Volcano Road one mile from the Volcanoes National Park entrance toward Hilo. The village has B&B's, vacation rentals, stores, a gas station, and restaurants like Lava Rock Café. Staying at Volcano House or in Volcano Village makes it easy to see the volcano at night and spend more time hiking and sightseeing in this unique area of the island.

Akatsuka Orchid Gardens is located on Highway 11 on the Hilo side of Volcano Village between the 22 and 23 mile markers. There are hundreds of orchids on display and tours are given of greenhouses where the orchids are grown. (Akatsuka Orchid website)

Akatsuka Orchid Gardens

Events and Festivals in Volcano

Annual Festivals in Volcano
Parade and Independence Day Celebration (July 4)

Volcanoes National Park Cultural Festival (July)
Volcano Rain Forest Run (August)

Regular Events and Activities in Volcano
Hula at Kilauea
Volcanoes National Park events
Volcano Art Center events
Friends of Volcanoes National Park events
Volcano Golf and Country Club
Farmers Market on Sunday morning at Cooper Center

CHAPTER 5: KAU

Southern coastline of Kau District

The district of Kau is on the southern slope of Mauna Loa Volcano with rocky coastlines, forests, pastures, and plantations. Many visitors to Hawaii Island drive through Kau from Kona on their way to Hawaii Volcanoes National Park and miss out on some incredible parks, beaches, and historical sites in the largest and least populated area of the island.

In March of 1868, Mauna Loa Volcano had an major eruption. Two earthquakes with a magnitude close to 8.0 and lava flows destroyed Kau farms and plantations. Fredrick Lyman, son of the Lyman missionaries to Hilo, lived in Kau at the time. He wrote in a letter to his brother that it was impossible to stand during the earthquakes. Even sitting on the ground, they had to brace themselves with their hands and feet to keep from rolling over. A tsunami caused by the eruption washed away entire villages along the coastlines of Kau, Puna, Kona, and Hilo. Mauna Loa covers half of Hawaii Island and is still an active volcano today. It has

erupted 33 times since its first documented eruption in 1843. Its most recent eruption was in 1984.
(hvo.wr.usgs.gov/volcanowatch/archive/1994/94_04_01.html)

The 40 miles from Kailua-Kona to the border of the Kau District at Manuka can take about an hour on the winding road with many sections of 35 mph speed limits. Once in Kau, Highway 11 has mostly 55 mph speed limits on the 50 miles from the Manuka Reserve to Hawaii Volcanoes National Park. Highway 11 is 1000 feet above the ocean through most of Kau and passes through the small communities of Ocean View, Naalehu, and Pahala.

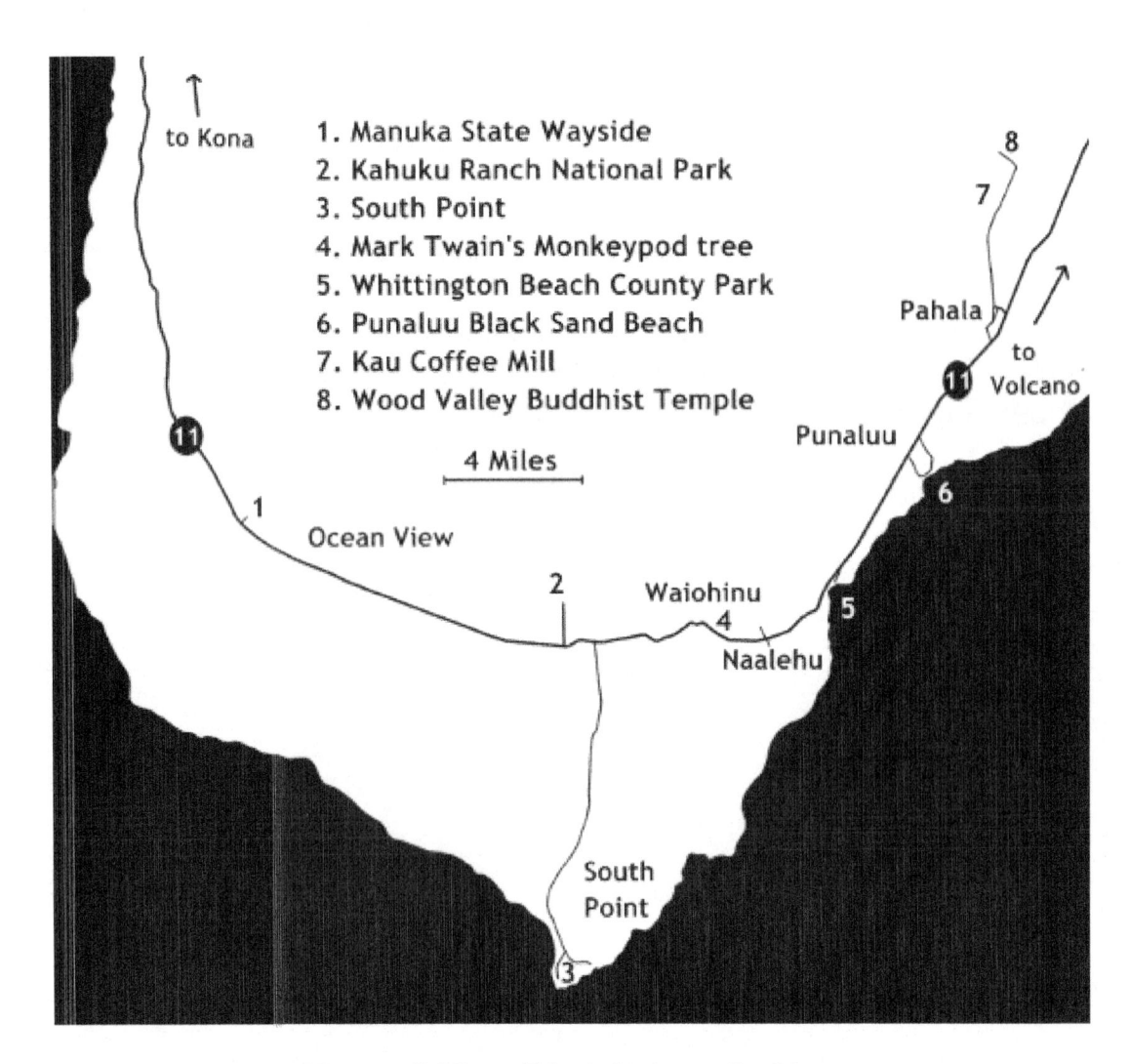

1. Manuka State Wayside
2. Kahuku Ranch National Park
3. South Point
4. Mark Twain's Monkeypod tree
5. Whittington Beach County Park
6. Punaluu Black Sand Beach
7. Kau Coffee Mill
8. Wood Valley Buddhist Temple

Map of Kau District and sites

1. Manuka State Wayside

Manuka State Wayside is in a 25,500 acre natural reserve on Highway 11 at the western border of South Kona and Kau Districts. The parking lot entrance is on the mountain side of Highway 11 between the 80 and 81 mile markers. The park has a nature trail, covered picnic areas, and restrooms.

The two mile Nature Trail starts next to the parking lot and passes through an arboretum with native plants and archaeological sites. The hike ranges from 1800 to 2200 feet above sea level on a path with areas of rough lava.

Manuka State Wayside Park Nature Trail

A one acre "Manuka comfort station" was set aside in 1929 for forestry field work and a ranger station. There is a story retold from a park ranger that lived at Manuka ranger station in its early days. A walled enclosure near the park was thought to have been a former house site. According to the park ranger, near the house site there were five mango trees and five graves made with lava blocks. Each grave had a perfectly preserved skeleton. The largest skeleton measured 94 inches from the top of the skull to the bottom of its feet (7'8") with bones that were very large in proportion and perfect teeth. According to legend the area was called "Kanaka-loloa", which means very-long-men, and was said to have been inhabited by people who were very tall. (Handy, 1972)

During the missionary William Ellis's trip around the island in 1823, he heard the story of Maukareoreo, a celebrated giant and attendant of King Umi in the 1500's. The Hawaiians said he was so tall that he could pluck coconuts from the trees and when he was in a canoe he could reach down and grab fish from the coral. (Ellis, 1827) Though stories of Maukareoreo may be an exaggeration, there is evidence that Hawaii had giants almost 8 feet tall.

The community of Ocean View is located south of Manuka Nature Reserve. It has a half dozen residential subdivisions that extend up the slopes of Mauna Loa and along the ocean side of the highway. The largest development is Hawaiian Ocean View Estates (HOVE) with 10,697 one acre lots developed in the 1950's. The community has grocery stores, gas stations, restaurants, B&B's and vacation rentals.

A scenic turnout on Highway 11 is 2.3 miles from Ocean View with views of the South Point area.

2. Kahuku Ranch Unit of Volcanoes National Park

Gate inside the Kahuku Ranch

Kahuku Ranch, near South Point, became part of Hawaii Volcanoes National Park in 2003. The 116,000 acres were used as a cattle ranch that extended to the summit of Mauna Loa Volcano. In the last decade, the cattle range has returned to tropical forests with native trees and birds. The park has well maintained hiking and mountain biking trails.

The entrance to the Kahuku unit of the national park is on Highway 11 between mile markers 70 and 71 just 0.9 miles from South Point Road. The parking lot is on the mountain side of Highway 11 through two white posts. The ranger on duty, near the parking lot, has maps and information about the area. The park is only open on weekends and closed the first Saturday of the month. Entrance is free. The lower parking lot has restrooms.

Kahuku Ranch parking lot next to old ranch buildings

A six mile graded gravel road in the park goes up to the park trails. The road is drivable by a regular car to the Palm Trail, about 3.5 miles from the lower parking area. At that point the road gets steeper and a 4-wheel drive is recommended.

Road to Palm Trail in Kahuku Ranch

There are five trails in the park. The Puu o Lokuana Cinder Cone path is a quarter of a mile up to the top of the cinder cone near the park entrance. A longer two mile Puu o Lokuana Cinder Cone Trail goes by tree molds and lava flows to an old airstrip. The Palm Trail is a two and a half mile loop through scenic pastures and lava flows suitable for hiking or biking. The Glover Trail is a three mile loop to the edge of a pit crater and through a rain forest. The Kona Trail is a 4.7 mile loop to the edge of a lava flow past an old ranching area. (Kahuku Ranch Trail Guide)

Kahuku was a vast land division known for its hardwood trees and diverse bird population. Kahuku koa wood was used to build King Kamehameha's battle canoes and the colorful birds were harvested for their feathers used for capes worn by the kings and chiefs.

Kahuku Ranch was started by Captain Robert Brown, a retired seaman who purchased the 184,298 acres from C.C. Harris in 1866. Brown had a small herd of cattle and constructed a stone ranch house. Previous lava flows from Mauna Loa over Kahuku reduced the usable pasture land to about 15% of the acreage. Two years later, Captain Brown and his eight children watched lava from the 1868 Mauna Loa eruption destroy their home. The ranch changed ownership many times, at one point becoming part of Parker Ranch in Waimea. During World War II, the US Army took control of the lower portion of Kahuku and created the Pakini Bombing Range. They also used the ranch houses for a radar station (Kahuku Ranch Radar Station and Base Camp). In 1947 the ranch was sold to JW Glover. After his death the property was sold to Samuel Damon in 1958 for $1.3 million to pay Glover's debts. In 2003, the National Park Service purchased it from the estate of Damon for $22 million. (nps.gov/havo/historyculture/upload/HAVO_AOA_part%202.pdf)

3. South Point (Ka Lae)

South Point also called Ka Lae (the Point) is the southernmost point in the US. The point has dramatic ocean views from steep cliffs. South Point is believed to be the first area in Hawaii settled by the Polynesians and the area has many temples and historic artifacts.

South Point is 12 miles from Highway 11 on South Point Road, located between the mile markers 69 and 70. The 35 mph paved road becomes a one-lane road after 3.8 miles which requires driving onto gravel to pass vehicles going the opposite direction.

Dramatic cliffs at South Point

The Pakini Nui wind farm, which generates 21 Megawatts, is located 7 miles from Highway 11 where cattle graze on green pastures. A parabolic antenna belonging to the Universal Space Network that tracks and controls spacecraft can also be seen along the road. At 10 miles from Highway 11, there is a fork in South Point Road. The right fork leads to the cliffs, Ka Lae temple, and a light beacon. The left fork leads to an abandoned military base and the trailhead to Papakolea Green Sand beach.

Take the right fork and drive to the end of the road. Although the road is paved, the parking area has steep drop-offs and broken pavement which must be carefully navigated. Next to the parking lot are high cliffs with wooden structures attached used for fishing and lowering boats. There are unprotected and unmarked lava holes with ocean water surging at the bottom next to the parking lot. Cliff jumping is popular but it is not recommended because of treacherous currents below.

Parking area at South Point

The white sand beach of the ancient village of Waiahukini can be seen from the cliffs of South Point. The village was located three miles west toward Kona. Artifacts from the area date back to 750 AD and there is evidence that the first people in Waiahukini were from the Marquesas Islands. In the 1750's, King Kalaniopuu, the predecessor to King Kamehameha and ruler during Captain Cook's visit in 1779, built a home in Waiahukini village. He died there in 1782. The village was a main thoroughfare for traffic between Kona and Hilo where canoes stopped and were carried around South Point to avoid the dangerous winds and currents. By the 1860's, the inland road was used more frequently for travel than canoes and many residents moved from Waiahukini. In 1868 the village was destroyed by the tsunami created by the Mauna Loa eruption. (Kelly, 1969) (Clark, 1985)

The actual South Point (Ka Lae) is south of the parking area where a metal light beacon is located. Many visitors look around the parking area and never walk over to the actual South Point. To get to the actual South Point, face the ocean and walk to the left end of the parking area where a dirt road leads along the cliffs.

Directly in front of the Coast Guard light beacon is Kalalea Heiau, a temple dedicated to fishing. Inside the temple's stone enclosure is a rock called Kuula, the god of fishermen. (James, 1995)

Hawaiian fishing Temple in front of light beacon at South Point

A sign in front of the temple points to where 80 holes were carved so the Hawaiians could tie their canoes to land and safely fish in the tumultuous ocean. (James, 1995)

South Point canoe mooring holes

The view from the southernmost point of the island is dramatic with waves from opposite directions crashing into each other at the rocky point.

Returning to the fork in the road at the entrance of the South Point area, the left fork leads to a bumpy, one lane road to the old Kaulana Boat Ramp. A half mile down the road, foundations and old concrete structures from a World War II Army base can be seen. At the end of the road is the trailhead to Green Sands Beach.

The Army had barracks for 10,000 troops stationed at South Point during World War II. Later the Navy built a station to track missiles launched from Vandenberg Air Force Base in California. In 1965 the base became South Point Air Force Station until it was closed in 1979. (Clark, 1985)

At the end of the road is a circle where people park their cars to hike to the popular Papakole Green Sand Beach, which is green from the mineral olivine. The beach is remote with no services, no shade, and no water. The hike to the beach is 2.5 miles each way on a rutted road with a 100 foot drop down the rim of an old crater to the beach.

4. Mark Twain's Monkeypod Tree

Returning to Highway 11, Waiohinu is a historic community 4 miles from the intersection of South Point Road. It was the site of the first Protestant mission in Kau in 1841 headed by the missionary John Paris. The town had many visitors and was known for its fresh water stream. (Kelly, 1969) When Mark Twain visited the town in 1866 he planted a Monkeypod tree which has become a notable site along Highway 11. There is a small area to park and view the tree next to a Macadamia nut orchard. The fresh water stream was redirected during the days of sugar cane production and most of the residents moved away.

The old sugar plantation town of Naalehu is a mile and a half from Waiohinu on Highway 11. Naalehu, which means "volcanic ashes", is the southernmost town in the US. The town has a Farmer's Market on Wednesdays and Saturdays next to the ACE hardware store at the center of town on Highway 11.

Mark Twain's Monkeypod tree on Highway 11 in Waiohinu

Hutchinson Sugar Plantation Co. was formed in 1868 by Alexander Hutchinson in Naalehu where sugar cane farms had already been planted. He brought in a small mill and called his company Naalehu Plantation. The plantation had several owners until C. Brewer & Co. took control in 1910. The sugar cane was transported to the mill by 70 miles of flumes supplied with water through tunnels. The Naalehu mill broke down and a new mill was built at Honuapo (now Whittington Beach Park) where a wharf was built to load the sugar on to ships. In 1920 the plantation had 500 workers. The Hutchinson's Kaalualu cattle and dairy ranch supplied food to the workers. Nearby Pahala built a hospital and schools to support the growing area. In 1948, the Hutchinson Sugar Plantation stopped fluming the sugar cane and switched to trucks. In 1972, Hutchinson Sugar Plantation merged with Hawaiian Agricultural Co. in Pahala and was renamed Kau Sugar Company with over 8000 acres of sugar cane. When sugar production stopped in 1996, hundreds of workers lost their jobs and many left the area. (Hawaiian Sugar Planters' Association)

Punaluu Bake Shop on Highway 11 in Naalehu is a popular stop for malasadas (a deep fried pastry bought to Hawaii by the Portuguese). The four-acre estate has a tropical garden, restrooms, and a large parking area. Across the street from Punaluu Bake Shop is Hana Hou Restaurant with guest rooms next door.

Driving from Naalehu toward Volcano, a scenic view point is 3.4 miles on the right side of the road. The view point overlooks Whittington Beach and the dramatic Kau coastline.

5. Whittington Beach County Park

Whittington Beach view from Highway 11 scenic view point

Whittington Beach is located off Highway 11 just past the 60-mile marker, 3.5 miles from Naalehu. A dilapidated ocean landing structure, a remnant of the sugar cane plantation days, is in the bay. A royal fishpond is located between the park shelters and the ocean. The park has restrooms and picnic tables. It is not safe to swim at this beach because of the ocean currents.

Whittington Beach Park was once Honuapo village. The village and its large coconut grove were destroyed by the 1868 tsunami. It was uninhabited until the 1870's when the sugar plantations installed a sugar cane mill and built a loading area. Honuapo Bay was dredged and a wharf was constructed by 1883. A railroad was built from Naalehu to Honuapo. The 1946 tsunami destroyed the landings and wharf and left it in ruins. The area became a county park in 1948. It was named for Richard Henry Whittington who was a County Road Supervisor in Kau. He had moved to Hawaii Island from California as a teenager and came to Naalehu to work at the sugar plantation. Whittington and his Hawaiian wife had a business in Waiohinu and built their home above the park. (Clark, 1985)

6. Punaluu

Punaluu Black Sand Beach

Punaluu is a lovely coastal area and county beach park located on Ninole Loop Road about 1 mile off Highway 11. Ninole Loop Road is 7.4 miles from Naalehu between mile markers 55 and 56. Ninole Loop Road passes by the Sea Mountain Resort & Golf Club,

Punaluu Black Sand Beach County Park, a historic church, and returns to Highway 11 at 8.1 miles from Naalehu.

Punaluu Black Sand Beach is well known for its fine black sand and frequent visits by green sea turtles (called Honu) and hawksbill turtles (called Honuea). The turtles feed and breed on the beach and are often seen sunning on the hot black sand. The park is open 24 hours a day and there is no fee. Restrooms, showers, drinking water, and covered picnic tables are next to the parking lot.

The Punaluu area was inhabited by ancient Hawaiians who built the Kaneeleele Heiau, a large stone temple above the bay. Punaluu has a fresh water pond, called Kawaihu o Kauila, protected by Kauila the turtle goddess. Kauila was born on Punaluu's black sand beach. Her parents created the fresh water pond with their flippers and after she hatched she lived in the pond. She played with the children in the village and watched over them. A plaque about the legendary turtle goddess is in the park. (James, 1995)

Kawaihu o Kauila fish pond next to Punaluu Beach

In the 1880's Punaluu Bay was a port town used by steamers, sailing ships, and canoes. A pier was built to load passengers and sugar from the Pahala Mill. The town had stores, a hotel and warehouses. Tourists on their way to see the Volcano arrived in Punaluu. As the inland roads improved, shipping became less important and warehouse buildings were removed. The cement landing was destroyed by the Army after the attack on Pearl Harbor to keep it from becoming a landing site by the Japanese. The town was occupied by sugar plantation workers and used by fishermen until a 1946 tsunami destroyed all the houses. (Clark, 1985)

Directly across from the Punaluu Black Sand Beach parking lot is a small dirt road leading up to the tiny, historic Hokuloa Church. The short walk up the ridge offers a beautiful view of the beaches below.

The small, open-air, Congregational Church is a memorial to Henry Opukahaia, the first Hawaiian Christian who was born in the area. Henry joined the crew of an American sailing ship in Kealakekua Bay in 1808 to escape the battles raging between the chiefs on the island. He studied in Connecticut and his passion to bring Christianity to Hawaii inspired the Church to send the first Christian missionaries to Hawaii in 1819, who arrived on the ship Thaddeus in Kona in 1820.

Hokuloa Church above Punaluu Black Sand Beach

Henry Opukahaia was born in 1792 near Punaluu. He fled the island after his family was killed and became a cabin boy on an American ship in Kealakekua Bay. Henry joined the Foreign Missions School in Connecticut and became the first Hawaiian Christian. He published his autobiography and wrote about the violence, idols, and Kapu religion in Hawaii. Henry died in 1818, a year before King Kamehameha's death, at age 26. He did not realize his dream of returning to Hawaii but his book inspired the first missionaries to come to Hawaii. The first group of missionaries arrived on Hawaii Island just months after the Hawaiian Kapu religion had been banned by the royal family. (Thurston, 1882)

The next town on Highway 11 past Punaluu is Pahala between mile markers 51 and 52 at Kamani Street. The Kau Hospital is at the intersection of Kamani Street and Highway 11. The Wood Valley area is accessible through Pahala via Pikake Street which becomes Wood Valley Road.

Pahala and Wood Valley were developed by the Hawaiian Agricultural Company. In the 1870's, a sugar mill from London was brought to Pahala, the largest in the islands at the time. By 1914, a flume system was installed to transport sugar cane from the Pahala and Wood Valley farms to the mill. Sugar was shipped from the landing in Punaluu. Pahala built schools, a theater and recreation facilities for sugar cane workers from China, Japan, and the Pacific Islands. In the 1960's, the sugar plantation owners diversified by planting macadamia nut orchards. (Hawaiian Sugar Planters' Association)

7. Kau Coffee Mill

Kau Coffee Mill (96-2694 Wood Valley Road) is a show room for Kau coffee. The store has a view into the coffee processing equipment area, coffee tastings, and coffee beans for sale. The mill is located on the Olson coffee farm and serves other Kau coffee farmers in the area. The store is open every day. Covered picnic tables and restrooms are located next to the store.

Kau Coffee Mill

From Highway 11 take Kamani Street 0.4 miles past the bank and Post Office to Pikake Street (Route 151). Turn right on Pikake Street and the mill is located 2.5 miles down the road on the left side. (Kau Coffee Mill website)

When Kau Sugar Company stopped production in 1996, over 8000 acres of sugar cane fields became available and the land was offered to sugar workers for farming. Kau Farm and Ranch Company purchased over 2,000 acres of the land and leased 280 acres to 40 coffee farmers. Since 2007, Kau coffee has won international competitions and gained a reputation for excellence. Kau coffee farmers claim their soil has a higher pH than Kona soil making the coffee more mellow and sweet. (Hawaiian Sugar Planters' Association) (kaucoffeemill.com)

8. Wood Valley Buddhist Temple

The Nechung Dorje Drayang Ling Buddhist Temple, which means "Immutable Island of Melodious Sound", is located on 25 acres in Wood Valley. The temple was established in 1973 and has been visited by the Dalai Lama. Visitors can walk around the grounds, join in daily chanting and meditation, or stay at the guest house. The temple welcomes visitors and requests a donation. (Nechung Temple website)

Buddhist Temple in Wood Valley

From Highway 11 take Kamani Street and turn right at Pikake Street (Route 151) which becomes Wood Valley Road. After 3 miles the road veers to the left past a stand of Norfolk pines, goes over a one way bridge, and makes a left turn into a heavy forest. Brightly colored prayer flags can be seen from the road where the temple is hidden by trees. The temple is 2.2 miles past the Kau Coffee Mill and 4.7 miles from Pikake street.

CHAPTER 6: PUNA

Papaya Plantation in Puna

Puna encompasses the southeastern portion of Hawaii Island from Volcano to Hilo. For generations, independent farmers have been growing papayas, oranges, bananas, macadamia nuts, coffee, sugar cane, and raising cattle. Affordable and fertile land has continued to attract people to the wet, tropical region. Puna District has 52,500 improved lots in large housing subdivisions located along Highway 130, more than half of the property lots on Hawaii Island. Though Puna is remote, its population growth is the fastest in Hawaii and is expected to continue to grow because only about one quarter of the lots in the district are currently occupied.

The legends and stories of Puna's rain forests, beaches, and fishing villages and their destruction by the volcano goddess Pele are told in ancient Hawaiian chants. Active lava flows are a constant threat to farms and homes in Puna.

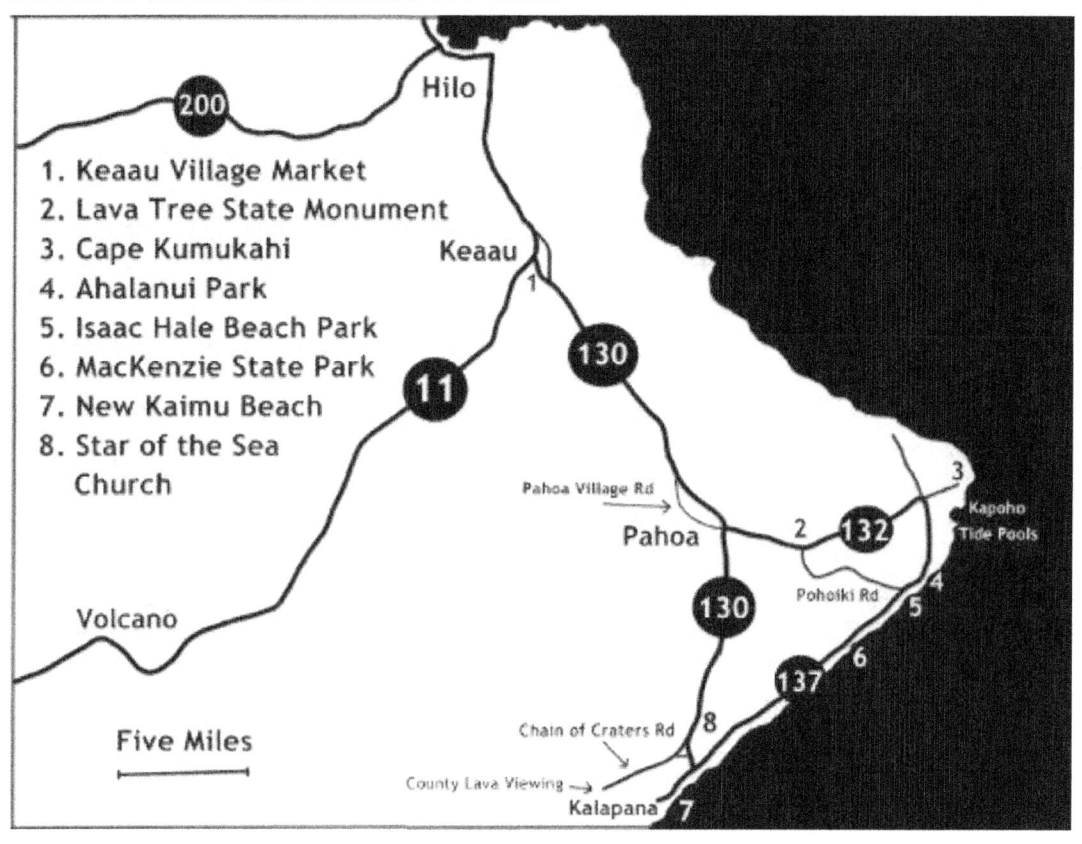

Map of Puna District and sites

1. Keaau Village Market
2. Lava Tree State Monument
3. Cape Kumukahi
4. Ahalanui Park
5. Isaac Hale Beach Park
6. MacKenzie State Park
7. New Kaimu Beach
8. Star of the Sea Church

Keaau town, once called Olaa, is located on Highway 11 at Keaau-Pahoa Road (Highway 130). A bypass of Keaau-Pahoa Road circles around the south part of Keaau and Old Volcano Road runs through the town. Keaau is a lively town with schools, churches, and shopping centers.

By the 1880's, WH Shipman and Rufus Anderson Lyman, sons of the early missionaries, owned most of the land in Puna. Shipman owned the Keaau land division from Hilo to the Hawaiian Beaches and Park subdivision. Lyman owned the Keahialaka and Kapoho land divisions.

In 1899, Olaa Sugar Company was started by Shipman, Lorrin Thurston, A. Carter, S. Damon, and B. Dillingham with over 30,000 acres of land. Coffee and ohia forests were cleared for sugar cane fields. The Hilo railroad transported sugar from Puna to Hilo until the 1946 tsunami shut down the railroad and it was replaced by trucks. Low sugar prices, bug infestations, and volcanic eruptions hurt profits and by the end of 1947, Olaa Sugar Company had huge debt. The plantation sold land to raise money. The company was renamed to Puna Sugar Company in 1960 and for a time had better luck. Though improvements were made and a power plant built, the sugar industry declined and in 1984 Puna Sugar Company shut down. The company gave five acres to each employee as part of their severance package. (Hawaiian Sugar Planters' Association)

WH Shipman Ltd., established in 1882, is still the primary land owner in the Keaau area. Herbert Shipman took over the Shipman operations in 1943 after his father, WH Shipman, died. He is known for breeding the endangered Hawaiian geese (nene) and growing orchids and anthuriums commercially. In 1948, Herbert Shipman sold some of the Puna land for a commercial macadamia nut plantation which later became Mauna Loa Macadamia Nut Corporation. Today the Shipman family owns 17,000 acres in Puna including a business park, shopping center in Keaau, and a private estate at Haena Beach. (whshipman.com/about-whs/history)

1. Keaau Village Market

Keaau Village Market fruit stands

Keaau Village Market (16-0550 Old Volcano Road) is a great place to sample Puna grown fruits and vegetables. The market also has baked goods and ethnic foods. The market is open Tuesday to Saturday and the parking lot is accessible from Old Volcanoes Road and Keaau-Pahoa Road. Restrooms are available.

From Keaau Village Market turn onto Keaau-Pahoa Road (away from Highway 11) and drive to the end of the road where it intersects with Keaau-Pahoa Bypass Road. Turn right towards Pahoa town.

In 1959, Herbert Shipman sold 15 square miles to David Watumull, who subdivided it to create Hawaiian Paradise Park (HPP) one of the largest subdivisions in Hawaii. Watumull retained over 2000 acres at Kings Landing near Hilo and owns Keaau Shopping Center and other retail properties in Puna and around the state of Hawaii. (Edwards, 1978)

David Watumull's father was Gobindram Watumull who came to Honolulu from India to assist his brother. His mother was Ellen Jensen, born in Portland Oregon, who lost her citizenship after she married Gobindram in 1922, due to a law that only applied to woman marrying Asian men. His mother helped lobby to change the law which finally happened in 1931. (Ariyoshi, 1998)

Between Keaau and Pahoa on Highway 130 (just past HPP on the Pahoa side) is the site of the largest Farmer's Market on the island, Makuu Farmer's Market. The market is only open Sunday mornings when a crowd shows up for the food and entertainment. Parking is free and restrooms are available.

Keaau-Pahoa Road has a fork (9 miles from the intersection of Keaau-Pahoa Road and Keaau-Pahoa Bypass Road in Keaau) with Pahoa Village Road to the right and Keaau-Pahoa Road, which bypasses Pahoa town, to the left. Take the right fork to Pahoa Village Road to see Pahoa's downtown and boardwalk.

The Pahoa settlement was originally a lumber mill where ohia trees were logged and cut into railroad ties. A spur of the Hilo train ran into Pahoa, "like a dagger into the forest", which it is said how Pahoa got its name. The wood ties were moved to Hilo by train and shipped to California for the Union Pacific and Southern Pacific Railroads. As the sugar cane fields expanded, the train transported sugar and molasses to Hilo and folks from Pahoa hitched rides on the train to attend school in Hilo. After the 1946 tsunami shut down the Hilo railroad, trucks were used for sugar transportation and Government Beach Road was the main route to Puna. (Edwards, 1978)

Pahoa Town boardwalk

Pahoa has covered wooden boardwalks and storefronts with old western and Victorian architectures on Pahoa Village Road.

2. Lava Tree State Monument

Lava Tree State Monument is located on Kapoho Road (Highway 132) 2.7 miles from the Highway 130 and Pahoa Village Road intersection. The park has a 0.7 mile paved path under a canopy of trees with about 85 unusual lava formations called lava trees molds. The lava tree molds were formed by a lava flow in 1790 that covered living trees and hardened. The loop takes about 30 minutes to walk. There are two shelters on the path that provide cover during rain. The park is open during daylight hours and has no entrance fee. There are restrooms next to the parking area.

Lava tree in Lava Tree State Monument

From Lava Tree State Monument continue on Highway 132, toward the coast, for 6.8 miles. The road passes through papaya plantations and at about 4 miles, red cinder can be seen along the side of the road. The red cinder was created by a 1960 eruption that engulfed the nearby town of Kapoho.

In January 1960, the ground in old Kapoho town split open and was shaken by earthquakes. Most of the residents evacuated. That evening, a fissure opened up below the town and lava spurted into the sky. The lava flowed toward the ocean and covered a popular resort called Warm

Springs despite efforts to save it by using bulldozers to move dirt and redirect the lava. Barriers were built to save Kapoho town as a red cinder cone formed taller than the buildings in the town. Ultimately, the entire town was covered in lava and all the homes, schools, and businesses burned. The lava flow stopped at the end of Cape Kumukahi in mid-February 1960. (hvo.wr.usgs.gov/Kilauea/history/1960)

Kapoho Road (Highway 132) ends at Highway 137, which is still referred to as the Red Road from the red cinder used to pave it. At the intersection of Highway 132 and 137, a dirt road across from Highway 132 leads to Cape Kumukahi.

3. Cape Kumukahi

Cape Kumukahi is the easternmost part of Hawaii Island with dramatic coastline views, tall sea cliffs, and a Coast Guard light beacon.

From Highway 132, drive across Highway 137 to the unmarked dirt road. The 2 mile dirt road is passable by a regular car and takes about 10 minutes to drive. The road goes past the old Kapoho cemetery and through a lava field from the 1960 Kapoho flow. It ends in a parking area next to the steel Coast Guard light beacon.

Coast Guard light beacon at Cape Kumukahi

    The cape was named for the Puna chief Kumu-kahi who was kind to the volcano goddess Pele when she appeared as a beautiful woman, but earned her wrath when he ridiculed her when she later appeared as an old woman. Pele flashed out volcanic fire and chased him to the sea where he was caught on the beach and covered with a mound of lava that extended into the ocean and created the cape. (James, 1995)

    Kumukahi is where the first sunlight touches the island and is considered a place of healing and mana (spiritual power). The temple, Kukii Heiau was located near the cape on an old volcanic mound. It is believed to have been built by King Umi in the 1500's and used for astronomical observation. It was considered so significant that in 1877 King Kalakaua brought some of its stones to Honolulu to be used in the foundation of his new palace. Now the temple is overgrown with trees, the rock walls are barely visible, and the view of the ocean and sky are blocked. (James, 1995)

Abrupt end of 1960 lava flow at the edge of the Light Beacon

In 1933, a seacoast light for Cape Kumukahi was funded and water tanks, sidewalks, houses for the keepers, and a foundation for the light tower were built. Due to frequent earthquakes a unique, reinforced concrete foundation was built for the tower which allowed a lower block to move with the earth without shaking the tower. In 1934, a skeleton tower was constructed of steel, and a beacon was placed on top of the 125 foot structure. In 1960 the Kapoho lava flow destroyed the light keeper's house and approached within a few feet of the light tower. For some unknown reason the flow went around the foundation and left the steel tower and foundation untouched. After the 1960 lava flow, the light beacon was fully automated. (lighthousefriends.com)

From Cape Kumukahi, return on the dirt road to the paved intersection and turn left on to Highway 137 (Red Road). Highway 137 goes past a residential area called Kapoho Beach Lots and Vacationland that surround a bay with tide pools. The Kapoho tide pools are a series of large interconnected thermal tide pools with some that extend 200 yards out into the ocean. The tide pools are accessible to the public from a small parking area. To get to the tide pools, turn on to Kapoho Kai Drive which veers to the right and ends at Wai Opae Road. A rocky, unpaved parking area is located at the end of Wai Opae and there is a charge for parking.

4. Ahalanui State Park

Ahalanui Hot Springs

At 2.6 miles from the intersection of Highway 132, Highway 137 narrows under a canopy of trees. The entrance to Ahalanui State Park parking lot is 0.2 miles after the road narrows, just past mile marker 10, on the left (ocean side) of the road.

Ahalanui State Park is a natural hot spring created by heat from the volcano. The large swimming pond is within a man made wall where fresh ocean water can flow in. Fish sometimes swim into the pool from the ocean and the clear water makes it good for snorkeling. The water can get up to 90 degrees Fahrenheit. The pond is accessible through staircases leading into the water and life guards are on site. The ocean on the other side of the wall is ferocious and not safe for swimming. The park is free and open daily. The park has picnic tables, grills, restrooms, and shaded areas to sit and enjoy the view of the ocean.

5. Isaac Hale Park

Isaac Hale Park and Boat Launch

Isaac Hale Beach Park is located a mile further on Highway 137 from Ahalanui State Park accessible from Pohoiki Road near the 11 mile marker. It can also be reached by a small coastal road, the first turn toward the coast about 0.4 miles from Ahalanui State Park. The park has a large parking lot, restrooms, a playground, and the only boat launch in Puna. The Pohoiki surf break is considered the best surf spot on the Puna coast. The popular park has a series of hot springs on the coast.

From Isaac Hale Beach Park, Highway 137 goes along the coastline under a thick canopy of trees with portions of the road only one lane. Cell service is unavailable. This coastline is best driven early in the day on weekdays when there is less traffic.

6. MacKenzie State Park

MacKenzie State Park is located on Highway 137 just 2 miles from the intersection of Pohiki Road. The 13-acre park has awe inspiring views from the tall cliffs covered with ironwood trees. Needles from the forest of ironwood trees blanket the ground along the cliffs. Lava tube openings can be seen along the cliff's edge in front of the parking area. The park is named for Albert J. MacKenzie, who was a forest ranger and planted many of the ironwood trees.

Cliffs at MacKenzie State Park

MacKenzie State Park is open year round. There are picnic areas and restrooms near the entrance. It is dangerous to swim at MacKenzie. The cliff's edge can be unstable.

MacKenzie State Park is considered the most haunted place on Hawaii Island. The park was built by prison convicts in the 1850's, many who are presumed buried in the park after dying of the heat and poor conditions. Residents have reported seeing ghosts of starved men carrying tools at sunset. Local legends tell of ancient Hawaiian warriors called "night marchers' on the King's Highway, called the Red Road in Puna. People have witnessed processions of flickering torches on the Red Road which runs through the park and heard sounds of drums and chants. Reports of hearing footsteps, music and seeing ghostly figures on the trail have been posted on the internet by campers and visitors.

Many residents refuse to enter the park after sunset or on full moons. (Hunt, 2009)

Highway 137 Kapoho-Kalapana Road

From MacKenzie State Park, it is 9 miles on Highway 137 to Kalapana where the road was covered and the town destroyed with lava in 1990. Along the way is Kalani Retreat Center, between mile marker 17 and 18. It has a gift shop and snacks in a building on the highway and a restored Hawaiian temple on the grounds. Kehena Black Sand Beach is located near the 19 mile marker but is not visible from the road.

In 1983, a vent called Puu Oo on the eastern ridge of Kilauea Volcano opened up. Its lava flows destroyed homes, covered roads, and buried ancient Hawaiian temples on the southern coast of Puna. Lava flows briefly threatened Kalapana in November 1986 and destroyed 17 houses. In February 1990, the lava flow to Kalapana resumed and after many starts and stops consumed the town and covered the beautiful Kaimu black sand beach.
(hvo.wr.usgs.gov/Kilauea/history/1990Kalapana)

7. New Kaimu Black Sand Beach

A parking area is located in front of the 1990 lava field across from Kaimu Corner General Store. A trailhead to the new Kaimu Beach is next to the parking lot. The 15-minute hike is on a red cinder gravel trail that goes across a stark landscape of lava that covered houses, roads, and Kaimu Beach. Parts of houses and cars can be seen under the lava field. Residents have planted coconut trees along the beach to restore the groves that were lost. New Kaimu Beach is not safe for swimming or even wading due to extreme currents and waves.

Path across lava field to new Kaimu Beach

From the parking lot of Kaimu Beach, Pahoa-Kalapana Road is 0.2 miles on Highway 137. At the intersection, turn left to return to Pahoa. After 0.4 miles, the road has a fork where a tsunami siren tower is located. At this fork, the old Chain of Craters Road and Pahoa-Kalapana Road merge to form Highway 130. Kalapana's painted church is located near the fork on the right side of Highway 130 (driving toward Pahoa). Hawaii County's lava viewing area is located at the end of the old Chain of Craters Road.

8. Star of the Sea Painted Church

The Star of the Sea Painted Church was built in 1928 by the Belgian Catholic missionary Father Gielen who painted the upper sections of the inside of the church. Years later, George Heidler painted the lower panels. Some of the paintings tell of the story of Father Damien de Veuster, now Saint Damien, who lived in Puna in 1864 before he moved to the island of Molokai and served the leprosy community. The painted church was moved from Kalapana in 1990 to save it from a lava flow.

Painted Church in Puna

The Star of the Sea Painted Church is located on Highway 130 across from a Noni factory between mile marker 19 and 20. It is open to the public every day.

From the church, it is 21 miles back to Highway 11 on Highway 130 which takes about 30 minutes depending upon traffic and road construction.

Finding Active Lava Flows

The current Kilauea Volcano eruption has been active since January 1983, however lava flows stop and start and frequently change routes. Before driving out to Kalapana, check with Hawaii County and Hawaii Volcanoes National Park to verify that the lava is actually flowing and where it can be seen. A recorded message of viewing conditions by Hawaii County is at 808-961-8093.

Hawaii County manages a lava viewing area in Puna at the end of the old Chain of Craters Road (Highway 130). A private security company staffs a security shed in the public viewing area from 3 P.M. to 9 P.M. if there is an active lava flow. A path from the parking area leads to a lava mound that serves as a viewing platform. The land along the old Chain of Craters Road and beyond the viewing platform is private property and public access is prohibited. The viewing platform does not always have a view of the active flow.

Path to Lava viewing area from parking lot

    While it may be tempting to walk to visible smoke from an active lava flow, unseen crevices and lava tubes on Puna's jagged lava fields makes a hike extremely dangerous, particularly after sunset. The safest option for hiking to an active lava flow is to take a guided tour. When the lava is flowing into the ocean, boat tours are offered from Isaac Hale County Beach park. Another option is an air tour from a helicopter or plane. Air tours are available from Hilo, Kona, and Waikoloa Beach.

    If the lava is flowing within Hawaii Volcanoes National Park, it can be viewed by driving to the end of the Chain of Craters Road within the park and hiking to the flow. More information about the current location of a lava flow and items you should bring on a hike are available on the national park's [website](#).

Events and Festivals in Puna
Annual Festivals in Puna
Puna Breadfruit Festival (March)
Puna Music Festival (May)
Puna Ohana Cultural Day – Makuu Market (August)
Keaau Christmas Parade (December)
Pahoa Christmas Parade (December)

Akebono Theater in Pahoa

Regular Events and Activities
Akebono Theater
Kalani Oceanside Retreat classes and workshops
La'akea Community permaculture classes
Kupukupu Center classes
Polestar yoga and activities
Kalapana Night Market Wednesday Nights 5 to 10 P.M.
Seaview Performing Arts Center events

CHAPTER 7: NORTH KOHALA

Mahukona Lighthouse in North Kohala

The north end of Hawaii Island is isolated from the rest of the island on the slopes of the extinct Kohala Volcano. The remote towns of Hawi and Kapaau are only accessible by the coastal Akoni Pule Highway (Highway 270) and Kohala Mountain Highway (Highway 250). There are no traffic lights or radio stations and even cell service is limited. When the Kohala Sugar Company shut down in 1973, the residents opened restaurants and galleries to focus on welcoming visitors.

Since the Hawaiians had no written language, the early life of Kamehameha has been passed down in oral stories. Kamehameha was born sometime between 1736 and 1758 (the date 1758 is popular because it coincides with Halley's comet). Kamehameha was born during the reign of King Alapai in North Kohala. Keouanui, King Keawe's grandson, is thought to be Kamehameha's father, but there is speculation that his father was Kahekili, the King of Maui.

Kamehameha's mother, Kekuiapoiwa II, visited her family in Maui before she returned to Kohala to give birth. She craved an eyeball which was considered a sign that the baby would become a killer of chiefs. King Alapai ordered his men to kill the baby, but a chief named Naeole carried the baby to safety and hid him in Waipio Valley. When Kamehameha was five, King Alapai heard about the child and had him join his father Keouanui in Hilo. (Lawrence, 1912)

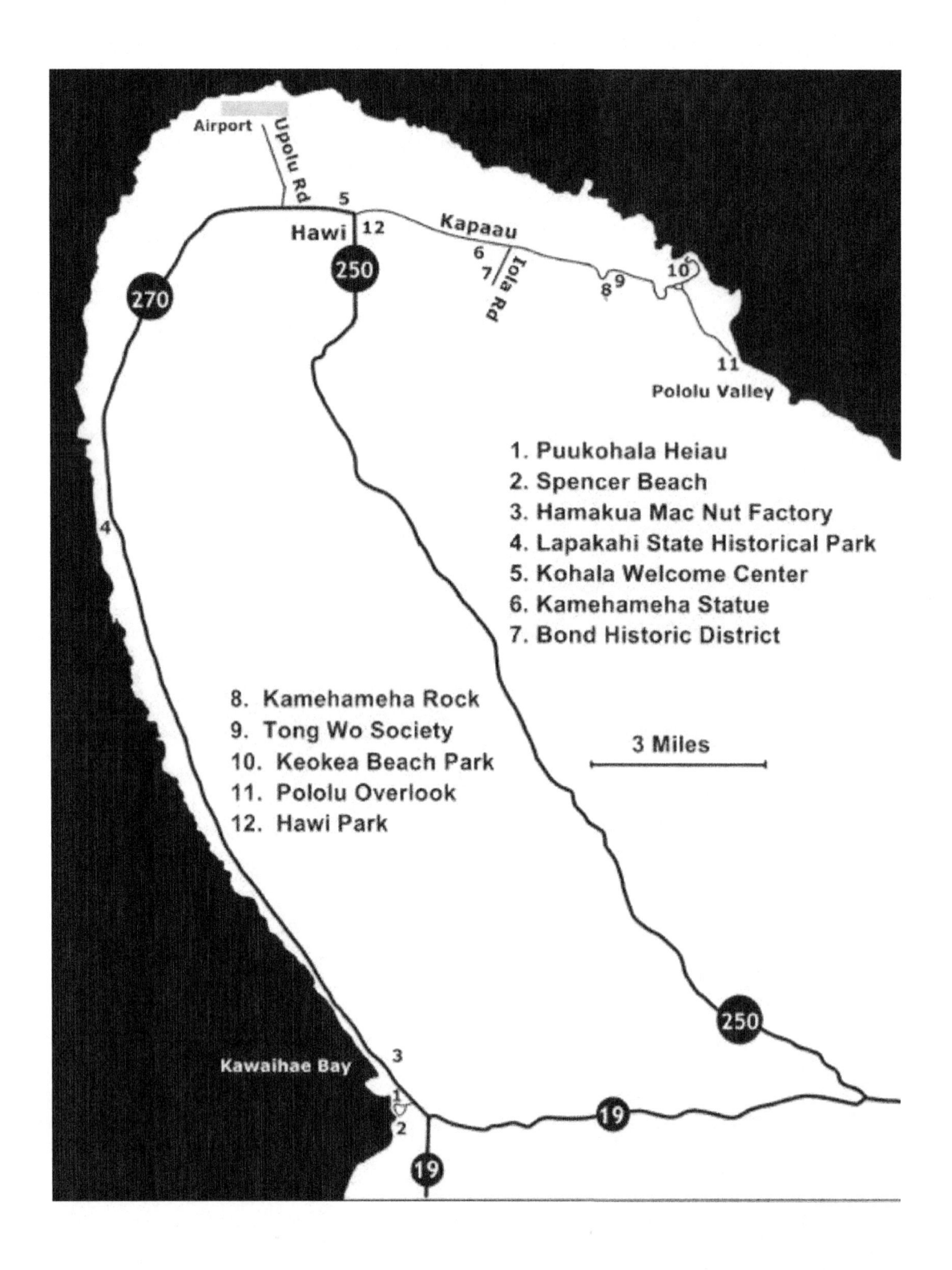

Airport Upolu Rd
Hawi 5 12 Kapaau
270 250 6 Iola Rd
7 8 9 10
11
Pololu Valley

1. Puukohala Heiau
2. Spencer Beach
3. Hamakua Mac Nut Factory
4. Lapakahi State Historical Park
5. Kohala Welcome Center
6. Kamehameha Statue
7. Bond Historic District

8. Kamehameha Rock
9. Tong Wo Society
10. Keokea Beach Park
11. Pololu Overlook
12. Hawi Park

3 Miles

Kawaihae Bay
3
1
2
19
250
19

Map of North Kohala District and sites

Akoni Pule Highway (Highway 270) begins where Kawaihae Road (Highway 19) and Queen Kaahumanu Highway (Highway 19) intersect. The road goes past Kawaihae Harbor and along the coast to the north end of the island where it turns east towards Hawi and Kapaau. The road ends at the Pololu Valley Lookout. It takes about 45 minutes to drive the 28 mile road with no stops. From the lookout, you can return to Kawaihae on Akoni Pule Highway or take Kohala Mountain Road.

Akoni Pule Highway is named after the man who made the highway a reality. Akoni Pule was a long serving Hawaii Representative who worked tirelessly to get funds for the North Kohala coastal route. He died before the highway was completed in 1973. Before it was built, the only way to get to Hawi and Kapaau was by Kohala Mountain Road from Waimea.

1. Puukohola Heiau National Historic Site

Puukohola Heiau National Historic Site (62-3601 Kawaihae Road) was established in 1972 to preserve the last major Hawaiian temple, Puukohola Heiau, built by Kamehameha in 1791. The 77 acre historic site also has an older Mailekini Heiau, which was converted into a fort to protect Kawaihae harbor. Hale o Kapuni Heiau, dedicated to the sharks gods, is submerged under water on the shoreline.

Puukohola Heiau entrance to Visitor Center

The Visitor Center has informative displays, videos, presentations by park rangers, and a gift shop The park has a half mile, paved loop path to tour the temples. Whales and black tipped reef sharks can sometimes be seen from the path. (Puukohola Heiau website)

Path in Puukohola Heiau National Historic Site

The Puukohola Heiau National Historical Site Visitor Center is located off Akoni Pule Highway (Highway 270) between mile marker

2 and 3. Turn toward the ocean after passing the sign "Spencer Park Puukohola Heiau NHS". The parking lot is the second right turn at 0.3 miles from Highway 270. The park has a small beach and picnic areas. Restrooms are located next to the parking lot. (nps.gov/puhe)

Within the park is John Young's house site where he lived until his death in 1835. John Young and his shipmate Isaac Davis were stranded on Hawaii Island in 1790 after the incident at Kaupulehu Beach (see Kaupulehu Beach in Kona Area Beaches and Parks). Young and Davis helped train the Hawaiians in western battle tactics and became trusted advisors of Kamehameha. John Young married twice and had six children. He lived at Kawaihae and met with ship captains and the first missionaries, who later wrote about him. John Young served as the royal governor of the island for 10 years and Queen Emma, the wife of King Kamehameha IV, was his granddaughter.

A powerful Kahuna (seer) told Kamehameha that war would end if he built a new temple for the war god Ku. In 1790, Kamehameha began building Puukohola Heiau above Kawaihae Bay. A human chain of up to 20,000 workers passed stones 25 miles from Pololu Valley to Puukohola to build the temple. While the temple was under construction, the northern coast had a surprise naval attack by the Kings of Oahu and Kauai who had recently occupied Maui and Molokai. Kamehameha stopped work on his temple to gather a force against the invaders. The first naval battle in Hawaii was called Kepuwahaulaula (the red mouthed gun) and both sides had western weapons. Kamehameha's warriors forced the invading army into retreat with the help of Isaac Davis and John Young who used a cannon salvaged from the ship Fair American. Kamehameha's work on the temple was later interrupted by an attack from the south by his enemy cousin Keoua. The Puukohola Heiau was completed in 1791. Keoua was invited to a peace talk at the site of the new Heiau at Kawaihae. When he arrived and stepped from his canoe, he was speared by a chief in Kamehameha's army. He became the temple's first human sacrifice. With Keoua dead, Kamehameha became the uncontested ruler of Hawaii Island. (nps.gov/puhe)

2. Samuel M Spencer Beach

Samuel M. Spencer Beach

    Spencer Beach is located south of Kawaihae harbor on the shoreline below the Puukohola Heiau National Historic Site. The beach is named for Samuel Mahuka Spencer, the Chairman of Hawaii County's Board of Supervisors from 1924 to 1944. The beach has white sand with a gentle slope into the ocean. It is protected by a reef offshore and harbor landfill on the north side. The beach has grassy areas, shade trees, and lifeguards. Facilities include picnic pavilions, showers, and restrooms.

    Spencer Beach is located off Akoni Pule Highway (Highway 270) between mile marker 2 and 3. Turn toward the ocean after the sign "Spencer Park Puukohola Heiau NHS" and drive to the end of the road where the parking lot is located.

    North of Puukohola Heiau is Kawaihae Harbor. At 1.5 miles from the start of Akoni Pule Highway, turn right at the gas station to continue north on Highway 270 toward Hawi.

Kawaihae Harbor

Kawaihae Harbor has a shipping terminal and fuel depot. A military landing site is used by the Army to land their 19-ton Stryker tanks for transport up to the Pohakuloa Training Area on Saddle Road.

When George Vancouver, the British Captain of the HMS Discovery first visited Kawaihae in 1793, John Young and Isaac Davis had already been living there for three years and Kamehameha had been ruler of Hawaii Island for two years. Vancouver left a letter with Young and Davis in 1793 recommending them to other sea captains as men who could be trusted and requesting that they be treated with civility and hospitality by any subjects of Great Britain and those of other powers dealing with them. In 1826, missionary Artemas Bishop wrote that Young had told him that he and Davis had "wandered from place to place dressed in the native habit, until at the suggestion of Captain Vancouver, Kamehameha gave them land."

John Young's popularity with Kamehameha gained him some enemies among the priests. A jealous Kahuna told everyone he was going to kill Young and went into the woods to build a hut where he planned to pray him to death. In response, Young built a small hut just opposite of the priest's hut to pray the Kahuna to death. The Kahuna became so worried and upset that he died which greatly increased Young's power and influence.

Young and Davis were indispensable to Kamehameha during his conquest for superiority over the Hawaiian Islands. They fought in battles at Hilo against the warriors of Keoua, in the naval encounter off Waipio under Keeaumoku, in the conquest of Maui, and in the battle of Nuuanu where Kamehameha defeated Oahu. With the help of Captain Vancouver's carpenters, they helped build the first keeled vessel constructed in Hawaii for Kamehameha's navy and they built forts on the island to protect against invasions.

Davis became governor of Oahu and helped negotiate peace with the King of Kauai which finally united all the islands. Davis was poisoned in 1810 after warning the Kauai King of a plot to kill him. Young was governor of Hawaii Island from 1802 to 1812 and his residence in Kawaihae made it a required stop for sea captains who obtained his blessing before conducting business with the Hawaiian government. (nps.gov/history/history/online_books/kona/history3.htm)

3. Hamakua Macadamia Nut Factory

The Hamakua Macadamia Nut Factory Visitor Center has glass windows with a view into the area where workers make candies and process nuts. Free samples and coffee are available in the store. (Hamakua Mac Nut website)

The Visitor Center is located at Maluokalani Street off Akoni Pule Highway. Turn right (inland) at the first street past Kawaihae Harbor (1.8 miles north of the turnoff to Puukohola Heiau). Drive 0.2 miles up the street to the entrance road which leads up to the parking lot. The Visitor Center is open every day.

Hamakua Macadamia Nut Factory and store

From the Hamakua Macadamia Nut Factory, return to Akoni Pule Highway, turn right, and continue to drive north.

4. Lapakahi State Historical Park

Lapakahi State Historical Park is a partially restored ancient Hawaiian fishing village on Koaie Cove. A self-guided tour on a stone trail consists of two half mile loops which lead past burial sites, a canoe house, reconstructed houses, a walled residential complex, and shrines along the shoreline. The trail is uneven and steep in some places. It is possible to walk down a dirt road to the coast to enjoy the ocean view and bypass the trail. Looking north, the white Mahukona Coast Guard lighthouse can be seen.

Lapakahi State Historical Park is located on the Akoni Pule Highway at mile marker 14, 11.7 miles north of the Puukohola Heiau turnoff. The park is open every day except state holidays. There are no park rangers. A brochure for a self-guided tour describing the 20 markers on the trail, plants, and other items in the park is available at the park. The brochures are in a receptacle near the restrooms in the parking lot. The brochure is also available online.

Lapakahi Historical Park trailhead

From Lapakahi Historical Park, Akoni Pule Highway continues north. Upolu Airport Road is about a mile before entering Hawi. The two-mile, one lane paved road ends at Upolu Airport. The airport is used by private pilots and air tour operators. A wind turbine farm is located along the road near the airport.

A dirt road at the end of the Upolu Airport Road leads to the remote Kohala Historical Sites State Monument where Mookini Heiau and the site of Kamehameha's birthplace are located. The area has no services and no cell reception. The two-mile rutted dirt road to the State Monument can become impassable in heavy rain, even with a 4-wheel drive vehicle.

Windmill Farm along Upolu Airport Road

Mookini Heiau is one of the oldest luakini type (human sacrifice) temples in Hawaii. Mookini was built about 1300 AD by a foreign priest, Paao, on the site of an older temple. Stories tell of the temple walls being raised from the height of 6 feet to 30 feet in one night by 18,000 Menehune, the legendary people, who passed stones hand to hand from Pololu Valley. (James, 1995)

Paao is said to have arrived in about 1295 AD from Samoa or Tahiti. He brought the Kapu religion, image worship, and human sacrifice to Hawaii. He brought alter stones by canoe from Tahiti and constructed temples where tens of thousands of men were sacrificed. Paao brought a new king to Hawaii from Tahiti, called Pili-Kaaiea, along with other chiefs and their families. They started a line of kings and all the kings and high chiefs of Hawaii later claimed they were descendants of Pili-Kaaiea. Paao's descendents became the Kahuna or priests. The last high priest, Hewahewa, prophesied the overthrow of the Kapu religion; he supported Christianity and the breaking of the Kapus in 1819. (Fornander, 1916)

5. Kohala Welcome Center

The North Kohala Community Resource Center (55-3393 Akoni Pule Highway) is located in Hawi, one block west of the Highway 270/250 intersection on the ocean side (across from Keau Huhu Homestead Road). The center has information about the area's history, activities, maps, and restrooms. (Kohala Welcome Center Center website)

Kohala Welcome Center in Hawi

Driving east past the Welcome Center, the town of Hawi has restaurants, galleries, and stores along the road. Hawi Road is the name of Highway 250 at the Highway 270/250 intersection. The town of Kapaau is 2.4 miles past Hawi.

6. Kamehameha Statue

The town of Kapaau is near the birthplace of King Kamehameha and a statue of Hawaii's great King is located on the grounds of the North Kohala Civic Center (54-3900 Akoni Pule Highway).

In 1878, King David Kalakaua commissioned an American sculptor living in Italy to do a bronze sculpture of King Kamehameha for $10,000. The bronze was cast in Florence and the sculpture was put on a ship for Hawaii. The ship sank near the Falkland Islands and the statue was lost. A new statue was commissioned and placed in front of the Iolani Palace in Honolulu in 1883. The original statue was found in a junkyard at Port Stanley in the Falkland Islands by an English Captain. He brought it to Hawaii and sold it to the King. The original sculpture was shipped to Kapaau, near Kamehameha's birthplace. In 1912, the statue was moved to its current location. (Langton, 1905) (Chapin, hawaiianhistory.org)

King Kamehameha Statue in Kapaau

The statue is located between mile markers 23 and 24 in Kapaau, 2.2 miles from the Highway 250/270 intersection in Hawi. The statue is next to the road which is lined with restaurants, galleries, and stores.

7. Bond Historic District

The 62 acre Bond Historic District at Iole Road is located a half mile from the Kamehameha statue in Kapaau. A wooden sign with "Bond Historic District" is at the intersection. Along Iole Road is an organic macadamia nut orchard and old buildings of the Bond estate. One half mile down the road is the Kalahikiola Church. The Congregational church was built in 1855 by Reverend Elias Bond and his wife Ellen. The church was badly damaged in a 2006 earthquake, but the congregation raised the money to rebuild the building. The church tower was repaired and the stone walls replaced with concrete. The wall around the church was built using the stones from the original church. (Kalahikiola Church website)

Kalahikiola Historic Church

Father Bond was a major figure in North Kohala. He and his wife came to Hawaii in ninth company of missionaries from Boston in 1841 They were assigned to Kohala where Father Bond traveled by horse to

Kawaihae, Waipio Valley and Waimea. The Bonds started a Boys School near the homestead and later a Girls School. Bond was the supervisor of roads, postmaster, school administrator, and land agent. In 1863, Bond started the Kohala Sugar Company, known as "The Missionary Plantation" to help create jobs and bring businesses to the community. The plantation was shut down in 1973. (newmoonfoundation.org)

There is an informational kiosk on the right side of Iole Road half way to the church. Six hiking trails through the historic district are open to the public.

The Hawaii Wildlife Center is on Pratt Road after mile marker 24 on Akoni Pule Highway and before Kohala Middle School. The center is a rescue, rehabilitation, research and education facility for native wildlife. They have a small gift shop inside. The center is located on Pratt Road past the Kohala Ditch Adventures on the right side. (Hawaii Wildlife Center website)

After passing mile marker 25, Akoni Pule Highway goes through a gulch. In the center of the gulch, along the side of the road is Kamehameha Rock.

8. Kamehameha Rock

Kamehameha Rock on Akoni Pule Highway

Kamehameha Rock is said to weigh 1000 pounds and have been moved to its location from Pololu Valley by Kamehameha to show his great strength to the men moving rocks to build Puukohola Heiau at Kawaihae. Kamehameha Rock is on the side of Akoni Pule Highway marked with a Hawaii Visitor's Bureau sign, two miles east of Kapaau.

9. Chinese Tong Wo Society Building
At the end of the gulch on right side is the Tong Wo Society building uphill from the highway. The Wo On building is in front of the Tong Wo building.

The Kohala Tong Wo Society was founded in 1886. The building is decorated with bright red and green colors and the grounds are well manicured. The building is not visible from the road, but if you park next to the Wo On building you can walk the short distance to the gate. Tong Wo is only open to the public on Chinese New Year's day.

Tong Wo Society building

The first Chinese came to Hawaii in 1789 to work on the sugar plantations and by the 1880's more than 1,000 Chinese lived in North Kohala. When a Chinese community became big enough, fraternal societies were formed for political, religious, and social purposes. The society buildings usually had an altar area for prayer, a meeting room, kitchen, sleeping quarters, and a nearby cemetery. Men gathered to gamble, play Mahjong, and smoke. The building was also used for meetings by the secret White Lotus Society that supported the overthrow of China's Manchu government. When the plantations closed on Hawaii Island, most of the Chinese moved away. The Tong Wo Society's building is the oldest Chinese building in the state and the only social center remaining on the island. (Chang, 1988)

After mile marker 26, the road narrows and there are three one-lane bridges before the end of the road. Just past the first one-lane bridge is Keokea Beach Park.

10. Keokea Beach Park

Keokea Beach Park is located off Akoni Pule Highway on the way to Pololu Valley Lookout. The park has an excellent view of the rocky coastline and a small man-made cove protected from the surf with a breakwater. Monk seals and whales can sometimes be seen from the shore. The turn off to Keokea Beach Road from Akoni Pule Highway is near mile marker 27. The 1 mile road leads to the beach parking lot. Facilities include a viewing area with picnic tables, showers, and restrooms.

Protected inlet at Keokea Beach

11. Pololu Valley Lookout

Pololu Valley Lookout is the gem of North Kohala. The Lookout has a spectacular view of the coastline and a black sand beach below. A small parking lot is located at the end of Akoni Pule Highway after mile marker 28 and 5.5 miles from Kapaau.

Between Pololu Valley and Waipio Valley are 24 miles of coastline with deep valleys. The six valleys from north to south from Pololu are named Honokane Nui, Honokane Iki, Honokea, Honopue, Waimanu, and finally Waipio. There are no roads and the rough trails through the remote valleys take several days for experienced hikers to traverse.

Pololu Valley Lookout at the end of Highway 270

From the Pololu Valley Lookout, return to Hawi on Akoni Pule Highway. The intersection of Highway 270 and Highway 250 is at Hawi Road. Hawi Park is on the left side, one block from the intersection.

12. Hawi Park and Kohala Mountain Road

Hawi Park is a grass square across from the Hawi Post Office with two large banyan trees. Over ten thousand acres of North Kohala sugar plantation land, the Kohala Ditches, and this park were bought by a Japanese Company, Surety Kohala Corporation, in 1989. The park is used for Hawi's Farmer's Market on Saturday mornings and Wednesday evenings.

From Hawi Park take Akoni Pule Highway (Highway 270) back along the coast to Kawaihae or take Kohala Mountain Road (Highway 250) over the mountain.

Banyan Trees in Hawi Park

Kohala Mountain Road (Highway 250) is a winding road, almost 22 miles long, that rises to an altitude of over 3500 feet above sea level and descends down to Waimea. The Kohala Ditch passes under Highway 250 at 1.1 miles past Hawi Park after mile marker 21. A Scenic Point is 14.4 miles on Highway 250 on the right side of the road. The campus of Hawaii Preparatory Academy (HPA) is on the east side of the road just before the road ends at Highway 19 in Waimea.

The Kohala Ditches were built to provide water to the sugar cane fields. Japanese workers blasted 44 tunnels and worked in dark, cold, and dangerous conditions while building the ditches. During construction, 6 men were killed and many mules. The Kohala Ditches were christened by Mrs. Samuel Parker at a ceremony in June 1906. The water flow starts at Honokane stream and runs through ditches, tunnels, and flumes for 18 miles ending in a 850 foot waterfall. (Thrum, 1906) Kayak tours are led through portions of the ditches near the Pololu Valley.

CHAPTER 8: WAIMEA

Grazing cattle in Waimea

The town of Waimea is located between the slopes of Kohala and Mauna Kea in the interior of Hawaii Island. The town is surrounded by Parker Ranch, one of the oldest and largest cattle ranches in the US. Waimea's cattle ranches and horse breeding operations became the center of paniolo (Hawaiian cowboy) culture and Hawaiian women's pau riding.

Waimea Town Map

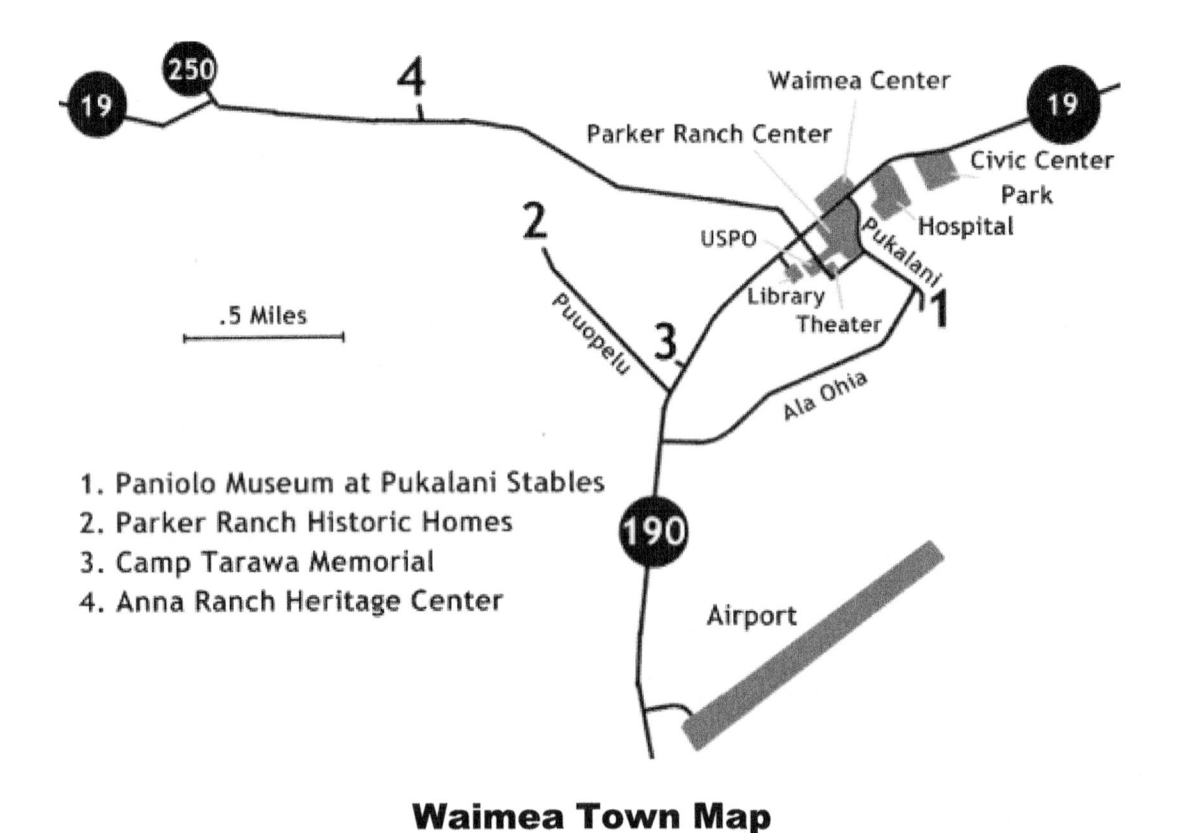

1. Paniolo Museum at Pukalani Stables
2. Parker Ranch Historic Homes
3. Camp Tarawa Memorial
4. Anna Ranch Heritage Center

Waimea is also home to WM Keck Observatory and Canada-France-Hawaii Telescope, North Hawaii Community Hospital, and several prominent private high schools.

Parker Ranch with Mauna Kea Volcano in the background

    In 1809, John Parker, a 19 year old from Massachusetts, arrived on a sandalwood trading vessel at Kawaihae where he jumped ship and hid in the forest. He became friends with the people living nearby and met Kamehameha who put him in charge of managing the royal fish ponds at Honaunau in Kona. After a couple of years he signed up with another ship on its way to China, but returned to Hawaii four years later in 1815. This time Kamehameha gave Parker the task of hunting the herds of wild cattle. Parker was the first person allowed to kill the Kapu protected cattle that roamed the island. The next year Parker married Kamehameha's granddaughter Kipikane and they had three children. Kamehameha made money from the sale of salted meat and hides to visiting ships and the growing whaling fleet in the Pacific. As the sandalwood was depleted, salted beef became the island's biggest export.

    In 1832, 16 years before California became part of the US, King Kamehameha III sent a high chief to Spanish California to hire cattle herders to help round up the wild cattle roaming Hawaii Island. The Espanoles (Spaniards) were called "paniolos" and over time paniolo was used for all cowboys in Hawaii.

    In 1847, John Parker purchased 2 acres in Waimea and he built a home he called "Mana Hale". The property was the beginning of the *historic Parker Ranch. (Brennan, 1974)*

1. Paniolo Heritage Center at Pukalani Stables

Pukalani Stables in Waimea

Paniolo Heritage Center at Pukalani Stables (67-139 Pukalani Road) is a museum of the Hawaiian Paniolo (cowboy) in the restored stables of Parker Ranch. In addition to the displays, the center has special events such as the monthly "Paniolo Talk Story" program and a Farmer's Market every Wednesday.

From Highway 19, turn at the stop light by Ace Hardware store on to Pukalani Street. At the next intersection there is a 'Private Road' sign that leads to the Paniolo Heritage Center at Pukalani

Stables. A parking lot is located directly across from the stables. (Paniolo Preservation website)

2. Parker Ranch Historic Homes

    The historic homes of six generations of the Parker Ranch family are open to visitors. "Mana Hale", built by John Parker in 1847, is a small two story koa wood house with a narrow staircase, and low ceilings. "Puuopelu" is a Victorian manor house purchased by John Parker II in 1879. The houses have heirlooms and everyday items once used by the Parker family. Richard Smart was the last Parker descendant to live on the ranch. Smart had travelled the world as a singer and actor before he moved to Waimea. Puuopelu house has his art collection and treasures from his travels. The homes are open Monday through Friday for a self-guided tour and 20-minute video. (Parker Ranch website)

Mana Hale built by John Parker

Puuopelu Road is located on Highway 190 just 0.2 miles from Ala Ohia Road and 0.9 miles from the intersection of Highway 19 and Pukalani Road. The homes are at the end of Puuopelu Road.

Puuopelu on Parker Ranch

When John Parker purchased his first 2 acres in Waimea, he was 57 years old and his daughter and two sons were already grown. In 1849 he acquired 640 acres of surrounding land and a year later another 1000 acres. Parker's sons, John Palmer Parker II and Ebenezer were heirs to the ranch. Ebenezer and his wife had four children before he died suddenly after swallowing a small bird bone. Parker's young grandson Samuel became heir of the ranch in his father's place. When John Parker died in 1868, Parker Ranch had grown to 47,000 acres and was split between 15 year-old Samuel Parker and John Palmer Parker II.

Samuel Parker attended school on Oahu, married Harriet Napela, and joined the high society of the royal family. The couple had frequent guests to the ranch in Waimea including the King and members of the royal family. While John Palmer Parker II managed his portion of the ranch and continued to expand, Samuel focused on politics and his lavish lifestyle.

John Parker II and his wife had no children, so they adopted the 4th of Samuel's nine children and named him John Parker III. In 1879, John Parker II bought a house in Waimea, called Puuopelu, and continued to expand the ranch. (Engebretson, 1993)

Since there are other Waimea towns on islands in Hawaii, the post office named, the town "Kamuela", for Samuel Parker, the grandson of John Parker. Samuel Parker's extravagant parties made Waimea on Hawaii Island known on all the islands.

Samuel's expensive lifestyle was a financial drain and his problems grew after a failed sugar plantation venture which forced the ranch to be mortgaged in 1887. John Parker III was 16 years old when he inherited half of Parker Ranch after the death of John Parker II in 1891. The other half was still owned by Samuel Parker.

John Parker III married Elizabeth Dowsett, introduced to him by Queen Liliuokalani. They had a daughter named Thelma, but John Parker III died two months later and his baby inherited his half of Parker Ranch. Thelma's mother hired Alfred Carter, a Honolulu lawyer, to manage the ranch. Carter moved to Waimea to restore and upgrade the ranch. In 1906, Samuel Parker sold his portion of Parker Ranch to Thelma's trust and the combined ranch was managed by Carter. In 1912, Thelma married Gaillard Smart and had a son Richard a year later. Thelma died in 1914 and Gaillard Smart died a year after that. Richard was raised by his Grandmother in San Francisco with summer visits to Parker Ranch. Carter managed the ranch until 1937 when his son took over management. (Engebretson, 1993).

Richard Smart had a career as a Broadway actor while Carter managed Parker Ranch. Richard moved to Waimea permanently in 1960. He expanded the ranch operations, built a visitor's center, and started a theater in Waimea. He sold and leased land for resort developments in South Kohala and the community of Waikoloa Village. When Richard Smart died in 1992, he left the ranch in a trust to help fund the North Hawaii Community Hospital, Hawaii Preparatory Academy, Hawaii Community Foundation, and Parker School. (prft.org).

3. Camp Tarawa Memorial

Camp Tarawa Memorial on Highway 190

Camp Tarawa Memorial is a metal plaque and three panel granite monument located at the site of a secret World War II Marine Base. The memorial is located on Highway 190 at 0.6 miles from the intersection of Highways 19 and 190 at Lindsey Road.

Before World War II, Waimea had less than 400 residents. Parker Ranch leased 40,000 acres to the US Marines for $1 a year. In December 1943, the Seabees arrived and set up electricity and telephone poles in Waimea. Three reservoirs with a capacity of 14,000,000 gallons of water were built. They constructed a movie house, ice plant, and many buildings still used in the town today. The streets were filled with convoys of jeeps, trucks, tanks, and amphibious landing crafts. Over the next two years 55,000 Marines trained at Camp Tarawa for their assault on Saipan, Tinian, and Iwo Jima islands in the Pacific.

The first marines to arrive in Waimea were survivors of the bloody battle at Tarawa, an island group which is now part of the Republic of Kiribati. After the battle at Tarawa, where almost a thousand marines were killed and thousands were injured, the marines landed in Hilo. They took the sugar cane train to Honokaa and were trucked to Waimea. The marines trained on lava, marched 12 miles down to Hapuna Beach to practice landing crafts, and used the Pohakaloa Training Area on Saddle Road to practice shooting their new Howitzer guns. Puuopelu house on Parker Ranch was used as the Marine Headquarters and a tent camp was located along Highway 190 next to the Camp Tarawa memorial. In April 1944, the Second Marine Division from Waimea invaded Saipan.

In the summer of 1944, the Fifth Marine Division from Camp Pendleton came to Waimea's Camp Tarawa to train for the invasion of Iwo Jima which took place in February 1945.

4. Anna Ranch Heritage Center

Anna Ranch (65-1480 Kawaihae Road) is a former cattle ranch owned by five generations of the Lindsey family. It has been converted to a museum and heritage center. Anna Lindsey Perry-Fiske was the last member of the family to live on the ranch. She died in 1995. Anna was a well known Pau rider which is a women's Hawaiian style of riding a horse.

Koa wood furniture, ranching gear, and family photographs are on display in the Ranch House, built in 1910. There is a self guided tour through the property and gardens on the Discovery Trail. A blacksmith and master saddle maker also work on the property.

Anna Ranch in Waimea

Anna Ranch is located on Highway 19, 1.6 miles from Pukalani Road when driving toward Kawaihae. It is open Tuesday through Friday. Reservations and a fee are required for the Ranch Home Tour. The Discovery Trail is free. (Anna Ranch website)

Pau riding is a Hawaiian horse riding style seen in parades on the Island. It is named for the pau, an elaborately draped divided skirt made from yards of material, worn by women sitting astride on horseback. The skirt protected women's clothes from dust and mud along the trails on the way to social events. Today pau riding is popular in island parades with women in spectacular outfits and garlands showing their horse riding skills. Anna's collection of costumes, hats, boots and saddles can be seen at the ranch. Her mother was a well known rider and Anna introduced pau riding outside of Hawaii at the Pasadena Tournament of Roses and Calgary Stampede. (annaranch.org)

Events and Festivals in Waimea

Annual Festivals in Waimea

Cherry Blossom Heritage Festival (February)
Parker Ranch Annual Horse Races and Rodeo (July 4)
Hawaii Horse Expo (August)
Honokaa UN Day of Peace (September)
Parker Ranch Rodeo (September)
Paniolo Parade (September)
Pumpkin Patch (October)
Waimea Christmas Parade (December)

Kahilu Town Hall in Waimea

Regular Events and Activities

Arts Council
Canada France Hawaii Telescope
Hawaii Preparatory Academy
Isaacs Art Center Museum
Kahua Ranch
Keck Observatory
Kahilu Theatre
Kohala Center
Parker Ranch Center
Parker Ranch Hunting
Parker School

CHAPTER 9: DRIVING HAWAII ISLAND

Driving around Hawaii Island is a great way to experience dramatic coastlines, different climate zones, incredible beaches, and rain forests. Hawaii Belt Road is the two-lane, 220 mile highway that circles the island and takes about five hours to drive with no stops. This chapter provides driving tips, estimated driving times, rest stops, and side trips to help plan island driving trips.

Driving Tips

The roads on Hawaii Island are somewhat different than roads and highways elsewhere. Below are some island driving tips.

Plan for longer driving times on the island. The island's roads have many sections with low speed limits (25-35 mph), sharp curves, and no pass zones. Road work, weather conditions, and wildlife on the road can also lengthen driving times. During peak times local commuter vehicles, delivery trucks, buses, motorcycles, and rental cars congest the island's few roads.

Slow moving truck between Honokaa and Waimea

Most roads have no street lights. In support of reducing light pollution for the optical telescopes on Mauna Kea, Hawaii County has ordinances to minimize outdoor lighting and requires the use of low-pressure sodium streetlights. The result is pitch black roads at night. During the winter, the sun rises after 6:45 A.M. and sets at

5:45 P.M. which leaves less than 11 hours of daylight to drive around the island.

Most of the island's roads are in unpopulated areas. In many places on the island there is no drinking water, food, gasoline, or cell service. In case of an accident or injury, dial 911 from a cell phone or use an emergency call box, located on some roads where cell service is not available. Carry proof of medical insurance, water, and emergency contact information.

Roads have multiple names and number designations. When roads on the island are given new names, their old names are often still used in addresses, maps, and road signs. One of the most confusing is Hawaii Belt Road, the name of the two-lane road that circles the island. This road is also called Mamalahoa Highway the name of the ancient island trail system. Hawaii Belt Road is designated as Highway 11 from Kona to Hilo on the southeastern side of the island; Highway 19 from Hilo to Waimea on the northwestern side of the island; and splits into two roads, Highway 190 and Highway 19, from Waimea to Kona. A portion of Highway 19 is also named Queen Kaahumanu Highway from Kona to Kawaihae and another portion is named Kamehameha Highway in Hilo.

Hawaii Driving and Safety Laws : Driver's licenses from other US states and countries listed in the Geneva UN Convention on Road Traffic are valid in Hawaii. Wearing seatbelts is mandatory for all passengers. All children under 4 years old must be secured in a Federally-approved child safety seat. All children between 4 years old and 7 years old must ride in a child safety seat or a booster seat (unless the child is over 4'9" or over 80 pounds). Drivers are prohibited from using cell phones or mobile devices while they are driving.

Hawaii has some unique road signs : Some of the signs seen on the road include: blue Tsunami evacuation route signs; blue emergency call box signs; yellow wild donkey signs; red, yellow, and white King Kamehameha shaped Hawaii Visitor Bureau signs (to point out historic sites); green Mile signs (mile markers); restricted 4-wheel drive signs; and orange steep grade signs. Signs with "Kokua" mean care or help and "Kapu" means no trespassing.

Driving Times Around the Island

DRIVING TIMES

A to J via Hwy 11   (119 miles) 2hrs 45 mins
D to J via Hwy 11   (95 miles) 2hrs 15 mins
K to P via Hwy 19   (56 miles) 1hr 15 mins
P to D via Hwy 19   (43 miles)   55 mins
A to J via Hwy 200 (95 miles) 1hr 55 mins
D to J via Hwy 200 (105 miles) 2hrs 15 mins

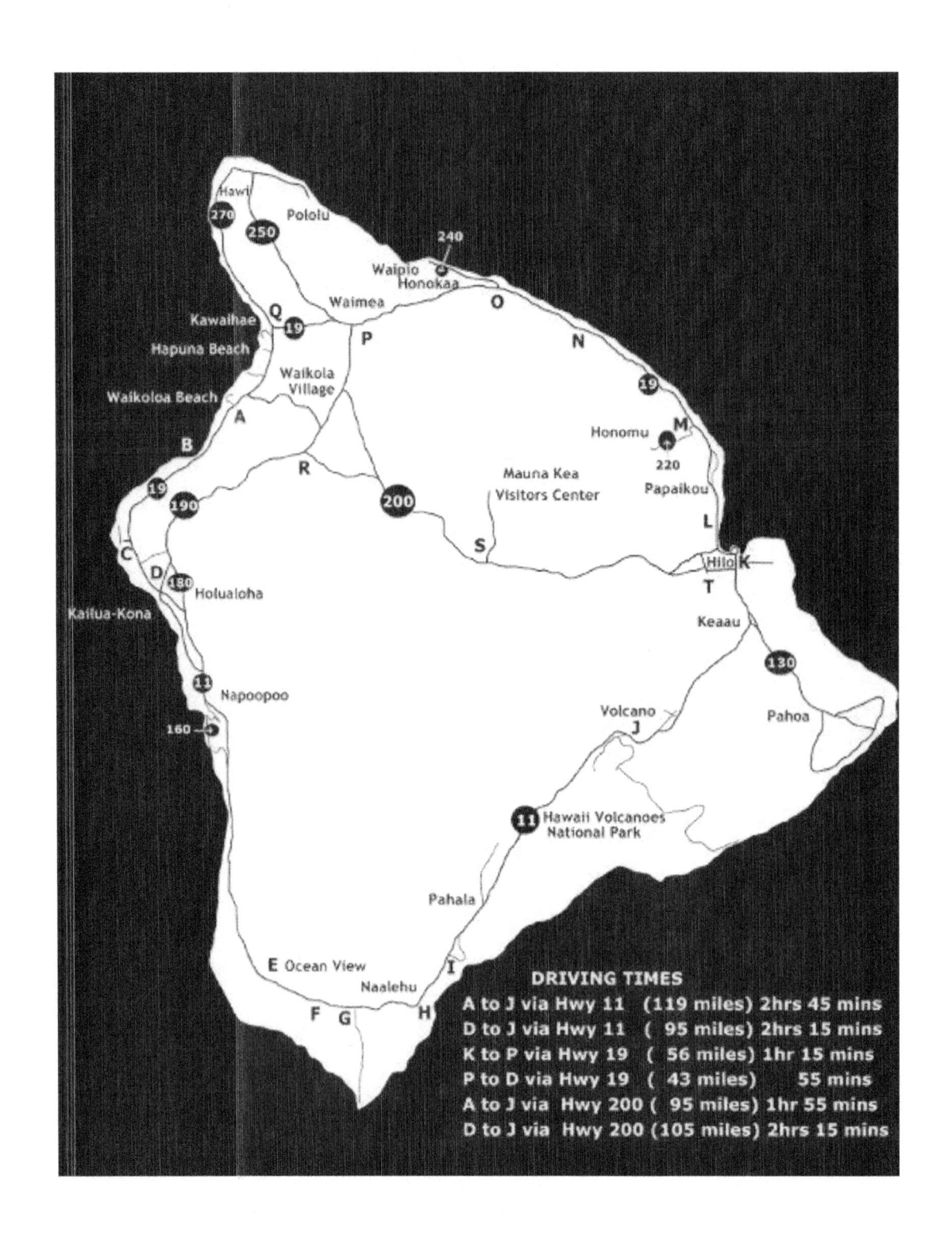

Island Driving Map (see TABLES OF ISLAND DRIVE TIMES)

TABLES OF ESTIMATED DRIVE TIMES

The tables below have distance and the estimated driving time between locations that correspond to letters on the Island Driving Map.

MAP ID	DRIVE AROUND THE ISLAND Via Hawaii Belt Road (Hwy 19 & Hwy 11)	Estimated Drive Times	Distance (miles)
A	Waikoloa Beach Resort turnoff (Hwy 19 & Waikoloa Beach Dr)	Start	0
B	North Kona Scenic Point	7 mins	6 miles
C	Kona Airport turnoff (at Hwy 19)	12 mins	11 miles
D	Kailua-Kona (Palani Rd & Hwy 19/11)	12 mins	7 miles
E	Manuka Wayside	1 hr 5 mins	42 miles

F	**South Point Scenic Point** (on Hwy 11 past Ocean View)	10 mins	6 miles
G	**South Point Road turnoff** (at Hwy 11)	6 mins	5.5 miles
H	**Whittington Scenic Point** (on Hwy 11 past Naalehu)	15 mins	8 miles
I	**Punaluu Black Sand Beach turnoff** (at Hwy 11 and Ninole Loop Rd)	5 mins	5 miles
J	**Volcanoes National Park Entrance**	35 mins	29 miles
K	**Hilo** (intersection of Hwy 11 & Hwy 19 & Banyan Dr)	40 min	29 miles
L	**Hilo Bay Scenic Point**	5 mins	2.5 miles
M	**Akaka Falls turnoff**	13 mins	10 miles

	(at Hwy 19 & Hwy 220)		
N	**Laupahoehoe Scenic Point**	15 mins	12 miles
O	**Waipio Valley Lookout turnoff** (at Hwy 19 & Hwy 240)	20 mins	16.5 miles
P	**Waimea Center** (across from Parker Ranch Center)	20 mins	15 miles
Q	**Kawaihae turnoff** (Hwy 19 & Hwy 270)	17 mins	10 miles
A	**Waikoloa Beach Resort turnoff** (Hwy 19 & Waikoloa Beach Dr)	10 mins	9 miles
D	**Kailua-Kona** (Palani Rd & Hwy 19/11)	30 mins	24 miles

MAP ID	DRIVE TO VOLCANO Via Saddle Road	Estimated Drive Times	Distance (miles)
A	**Waikoloa Beach Resort turnoff** (Hwy 19 & Waikoloa Beach Dr)	Start	0
R	**Saddle Road** (via Waikoloa Rd) (at intersection Hwy 190 & Hwy 200)	20 mins	16 miles
D	**Kailua-Kona** (Palani Rd & Hwy 19)	start	0
R	**Saddle Road** (via Hwy 190) (at intersection Hwy 190 & Hwy 200)	30 mins	25 miles

S	**Mauna Kea Access Road**	25 mins	23.5 mi
T	**Hilo** (Hwy 2000 & Komohana St)	35 mins	26.5 mi
J	**Volcanoes National Park**	40 mins	28 miles

Saddle Road and Mauna Kea

Saddle Road (Highway 200) towards Hilo

Saddle Road (Highway 200) is the shortest distance across Hawaii Island between the slopes of Mauna Kea and Mauna Loa Volcanoes. The Army's Pohakuloa Training Area (PTA), Mauna Kea State Park, and the Onizuka International Astronomy Visitor's

Center are only accessible from Saddle Road. The 50 mile road from Highway 190 (the upper road between Kona and Waimea) to Komohana Street in Hilo rises to an elevation of 6,632 feet.

Some car rental companies do not allow their cars to be driven on Saddle Road because there are no service stations on the road and freezing temperatures are common in the winter. Emergency call boxes are located along the road in areas with no cell phone service. During storms, heavy cloud cover can affect visibility and wildlife can be a hazard on the road.

Saddle Road can be accessed in two places on Highway 190, however the newest portion of Saddle Road called the Daniel K. Inouye Highway is wider and in much better condition. It is located 24.8 miles from Kailua-Kona on Highway 190. The older portion of Saddle Road that connects to Highway 190 is closer to Waimea and located 32.4 miles from Kailua-Kona. Saddle Road is accessible on the Hilo side from Komohana Street. To get there from Highway 11 in Hilo, take W. Puainako Street for 1.6 miles to Komohana Street then turn right and take the first left turn on to Saddle Road. The Saddle Road entrance in Hilo is called Highway 2000 and Puainako Street because the designation of Highway 200 was previously given to Kaumana Street and Waianuenue Avenue.

Snow covered Mauna Kea summit with international telescopes

Onizuka Center for International Astronomy is located six miles above Saddle Road on Mauna Kea Access Road. The Visitor's Center, at an altitude of 9200 feet, has displays, video presentations, gift store, and restrooms. There are hiking trails near the center and a stargazing program. (Onizuka Center website)

Mauna Kea Access Road is located 23.3 miles from the intersection of Highway 190 and the Daniel K. Inouye Highway.

Onizuka Center from above

Mauna Kea summit and the international telescopes are located at an elevation of almost 14,000 feet and only accessible by a steep, gravel road next to the Onizuka Center. The road to the summit requires a four-wheel drive and there are no services or restrooms at the summit.

If you plan to drive to the summit, it is strongly advised to spend at least 30 minutes at the Onizuka Center to adjust to the higher altitude. The Onizuka Center has weekly escorted caravan tours to the summit which you can join if you have a four-wheel drive vehicle.

Mauna Kea weather, road conditions, visitor information and guides are available online.

Island Side Trips

Two exceptional side trips along Hawaii Belt Road (Highway 19) are located between Hilo and Waimea.

Laupahoehoe Point Park

The Hamakua Coast, called the land of tall cliffs, can be seen close up from a beautiful park located below the cliffs in Laupahoehoe. The grassy park is at sea level with crashing surf and spectacular views of the coastline. The park has picnic tables, showers, and restrooms.

Laupahoehoe Harbor at the Point

Laupahoehoe Point was an ancient canoe landing site and later became a harbor for schooners and steamships. In the 1940's the point had a school, church, and homes. (Clark, 1985) On April 1st, 1946 the tsunami that destroyed Hilo's bayfront covered Laupahoehoe Point with 20 foot waves that killed 32 people, (23 students and 4 teachers). A monument for the students that lost their lives is in the Laupahoehoe Point County Park at the site of the school.

Laupahoehoe Point Road is the turnoff to Laupahoehoe Point County Park, located between Hilo and Honokaa. It is 26.5 miles from Hilo (about 36 minutes) and 14.5 miles from Honokaa (about 17 minutes). The park is 1.7 miles down a cliff on a narrow, twisting, road to the coast.

Waipio Valley Lookout

Waipio Valley, with a six mile shoreline, is the largest and oldest valley on the island. From the Waipio Lookout there is a breathtaking view of the valley's black sand beach and 1000 foot cliffs. The beauty and serenity of Waipio Valley has been the subject of many Hawaiian songs and has inspired writers and photographers.

Waipio Valley Lookout

From Highway 19, the Waipio Valley Lookout is 9.6 miles on Highway 240 (20 minutes) from the Honokaa exit. Highway 240 passes through Honokaa, an old sugar plantation town, and ends at a small parking lot. A path from the parking area leads to the Waipio Valley Lookout and restrooms.

Honokaa Town

The narrow road leading down into Waipio Valley is next to the lookout parking lot. A four-wheel drive vehicle is required for the very steep road (25% grade). There are no services available in Waipio Valley.

Ancient Hawaiians built fishponds, temples, and a place of refuge in the Waipio Valley. The soil was rich and crops grew well. King Umi's royal court was in Waipio Valley during the 1500's until he moved it to Kailua-Kona. The temples were visited by the Kings and Kamehameha received the guardianship of the war god, Ku by King Kalaniopuu at a temple in Waipio. Frequent flooding and tsunamis have reduced the productivity of the soil in the valley.

CHAPTER 10: PLANNING YOUR IDEAL VACATION

Mauna Kea Beach

When planning your ideal vacation to Hawaii Island, it is helpful to consider where you want to spend most of your time. If you are setting up snorkel, scuba diving, whale watching, fishing, or kayak adventures every day, then staying in town near tour pick up areas will save time driving to the activities. If your plan is to luxuriate on a sunny beach every day, a remote beach front resort may be the perfect place to stay. If you want to mix adventures and relaxation, it might be best to stay in several places.

An Ideal Time to Visit

Availability and prices of lodging on the island are very different between high season, when the island has the greatest number of visitors, and off-season. The ideal time to visit is during off-season when the island is less crowded and prices are lower.

December 15th to April 15th (High Season)
Most crowded and most expensive time
Holidays: Christmas, New Years Day, Martin Luther King Day, Presidents Day, Prince Kuhio Day

April 15th to June 15th (Low Season)
Less crowds and prices are down from high season; college students arrive for Spring break
Holidays: Good Friday, Memorial Day, King Kamehameha Day

June 15th to August 30th (High Season)
More crowded and prices are up from low season; visitors with school age children arrive
Holidays: Independence Day, Hawaii Admissions Day

September 1st to December 15th (Low Season)
Least crowded and lowest prices
Holidays: Labor Day, Discovery Day, Veterans Day, Thanksgiving

Hawaii has two seasons, winter and summer, with different weather and ocean conditions.

WINTER: November to April
Average temperature at sea level is 78 degrees; there may be snow on Mauna Kea and Mauna Loa
Coolest temperatures: February and March
Wettest time of year, resorts in South Kohala are in desert climate zones and mostly dry all year
Lowest ocean temperature is 73 degrees
Ocean swells on the north and west facing beaches; however storms can arrive at any time and create dangerous surf
Whales arrive in December and leave in April.

SUMMER: May to October
Average temperature at sea level is 85 degrees
Warmest temperatures: August and September
Highest ocean temperature is 80 degrees
Calm ocean, clear water, although storms can arrive at any time

An Ideal Place to Stay

Knowing your key desires in vacation accommodations (such as price, AC, kitchen, ocean view, swimmable beach, pool, and proximity to activities) helps to pick the ideal place to stay on the island. The large size of the island makes location an important consideration when selecting a resort, condo, or vacation rental. There are a limited number of rooms and vacation rentals on Hawaii Island. According to the Hawaii Tourism Authority, Hawaii Island has 7,660 hotel and condo hotel rooms as compared to Oahu Island with 31,400 rooms and Maui Island with 11,600 rooms. Hawaii Island's B&Bs and individual owned vacation units are an alternative to the limited number of hotel and resort rooms. When setting up your vacation, it is best to reserve cancellable hotel rooms and a rental car before you buy non-refundable airline tickets. People who buy their airfare first, often find island hotels full (which is why the airfare is cheap) and have to stay somewhere remote from their desired activities.

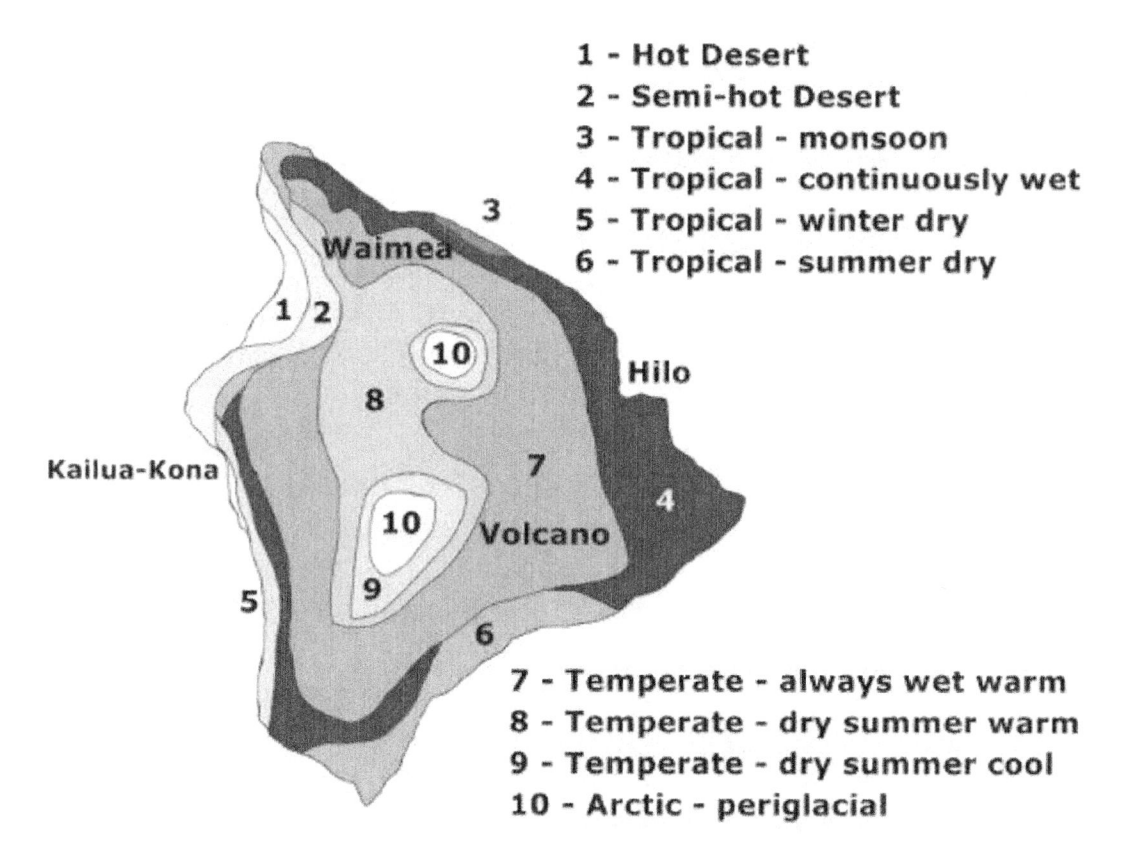

Hawaii Island Climate Zones [Jurvik, et al (1978)]

1 - Hot Desert
2 - Semi-hot Desert
3 - Tropical - monsoon
4 - Tropical - continuously wet
5 - Tropical - winter dry
6 - Tropical - summer dry
7 - Temperate - always wet warm
8 - Temperate - dry summer warm
9 - Temperate - dry summer cool
10 - Arctic - periglacial

Although two thirds of Hawaii Island is in a temperate climate zone, only the towns of Volcano and Waimea have places to stay in this climate zone. Most of the island's residents live in tropical climate zones with lots of rain. The resorts are located in the island's dry climate zones with more sunny days. The resorts in South Kohala offer the most amenities, but they are 35 minutes or longer from ocean activities in Kona. If you want to experience remote areas of the island, there are B&B's and vacation rentals in tropical rain forests, next to waterfalls, and along the rough lava coast on the east side of Hawaii Island.

Where to Eat

Visitors are often frustrated with the slow service and high prices of food on the island during the high season. The number of visitors staying in the Kona area varies from 70,000 to 120,000 a month between the seasons. Restaurants that struggle with throngs of hungry, impatient visitors during the busy months are often empty at other times of the year. To satisfy tourist tastes, most restaurants serve meats, potatoes, eggs, breads, and dairy products shipped to the island from thousands of miles away. The island's shortage of labor and the cost of food transportation greatly increases the prices of food in restaurants and grocery stores.

The best way to reduce the high cost of meals is to eat local food from Hawaii Island. The local fish, grass-fed beef, fruits, nuts, and vegetables from Hawaii Island are delicious and cost less than imported foods. They can be found at the island's Farmer's Markets and Hawaii owned grocery stores (Foodland and KTA). Self-serve restaurants and grocery store delis tend to use more local ingredients and require less labor. Cooking your own meals with local foods is another way to reduce the cost of meals.

For those looking for a romantic meal with spectacular views, Hawaii Island has some the best ocean front restaurants in the state. Menus and cooks change frequently. Online rating sites are the best way to find current restaurant reviews of the food, service, and prices. (yelp.com, urbanspoon.com, opentable.com)

Tips for Having Fun and Great Memories

Leave your valuables at home: Jewelry can be lost or ruined when swimming in the ocean and with all the activities and things to do it is easy to lose track of your valuables.

Don't get burned: Be compulsive about putting sunscreen on all the time. A bad sunburn can ruin a vacation. Find a high quality sun screen that is easy to put on and before you arrive test it to make sure it doesn't irritate your skin. Bring or buy a good hat with a wide brim to avoid getting a sunburn on your neck, ears, or face.

Be careful of the ocean: Never turn your back to ocean. Hawaii is famous for freak waves appearing out of nowhere. If you are in the ocean always face the surf and be prepared to avoid a big wave. Swim at beaches with lifeguards and get out when the surf gets dangerous.

Bring home great pictures: If you buy a new digital camera for the trip, get it early enough to learn how to use it before your vacation. When the whales are breaching or there is a perfect sunset, you won't want to miss it while you are trying to figure out how to take a picture with your new camera.

Printed in Great Britain
by Amazon